Praise for L

"*Dying in Islam, Rising in Ch...* by Cedric [aka Swidiq] Kanana with Benjamin Fischer, is like returning to the Acts of the Apostles. Here is the riveting autobiography of Cedric Kanana testifying to the power of the Lord Jesus Christ over Islam, African witch doctors, and even death. In the Lord's good pleasure he took Cedric, a born leader, captive from his spiritual enemies to bring honor to the name of Jesus Christ. A serendipity of this stirring narrative is its insights into a gang of thieves, the drug culture, Islam, and witchcraft. The only flaw in this book is that it has a last page. I hated to put it down. Thank God for our authors for giving us such a spiritually revitalizing story."
- *Dr. Bruce Waltke, Distinguished Professor Emeritus of Old Testament at Knox Theological Seminary and Professor Emeritus of Old Testament Studies at Regent College*

"All across the Global South, [God] is using his faithful people to speak and work in power — healing the sick, driving out demons, and reconciling mortal enemies. Rev. Cedric's story is distinctive in that it combines all of these marvelous works of God.... Hundreds of people have committed to following Jesus through Cedric's testimony and preaching, and it is my hope that this book will also be a tool for many others to place their trust in the Almighty God."
- *Most Rev. Dr. Onesphore Rwaje, Archbishop of the Anglican Church of Rwanda, Bishop of Gasabo Diocese, and Member of the Global South Primates Council*

"This story takes us on an improbable journey – which gives hope for our own improbable journeys. While the details of our lives may be different, Cedric's story of grace and transformation by Jesus will resonate with all who seek to know their true identity as a son or daughter of the king of kings."
- *Rt. Rev. Kenneth Ross, Bishop of the Diocese of the Rocky Mountains in the Anglican Church of North America*

"Cedric Kanana's remarkable story takes readers from the sordid depths of human darkness—the most brutal extremes of sin and even death itself — to the glorious, redeeming light of Christ. It is not an exaggeration to say that even the Apostle Paul's conversion was not as dramatic as this. I was mesmerized and inspired as I read the book."
- *Dr James Spiegel, Professor of Philosophy at Taylor University and author of* Gum, Geckos, and God

"As I have seen when Cedric shares his story in ministry, I trust this book will be an important help for both Christians and non-Christians as a way to recognize that many of our problems result from how we misalign our lives and place our hopes in things that betray or destroy us. Only Jesus could have saved Cedric, and only Jesus can save any of us."

– *Rt. Rev. Emmanuel Ngendahayo, Bishop of Byumba Diocese in the Anglican Church of Rwanda*

"This remarkable testimony is a vivid demonstration of the depths into which sin and error can take us – and of the amazing grace of God, who can save anyone, no matter how low they have sunk. It will introduce Western Christians to an unfamiliar world, but it speaks of the same Lord, who is wonderfully at work on every continent to bring people from all backgrounds and faiths to himself."

– *Vaughan Roberts, Rector of St. Ebbes, Oxford, and Director of the Proclamation Trust, as well as author of* God's Big Picture

"*Dying in Islam, Rising in Christ* is a testimony of a Muslim leader who experienced a powerful encounter with the Lord Jesus Christ. This man's story magnifies Jesus's words in John 10:16: 'I have other sheep that are not of this fold. I must bring them, and they will listen to my voice.'"

– *Dr. Lyle Dorsett, Billy Graham Professor of Evangelism at Beeson Seminary, pastor of Christ the King Anglican Church, and author of* Seeking the Secret Place: The Spiritual Formation of C.S. Lewis

"I first heard Cedric's story by the shores of Lake Kivu in Rwanda and marveled at God's incredible rescue and powerful grace. Since then, it has been my joy to witness how God has mentored Cedric as an evangelist – standing by his side, giving him the opportunity to boldly proclaim the gospel for all to hear (2 Timothy 4:17). May this account of God's work in and through Cedric be a further testimony of God's faithfulness to Africa and the world."

– *Blair T. Carlson, Anglican Minister, founder of GoodWORD Partnership, and former Congress Director for the Third Lausanne Congress: Capetown 2010*

DYING IN ISLAM, RISING IN CHRIST

Encountering Jesus Beyond the Grave

DYING IN ISLAM, RISING IN CHRIST
Encountering Jesus Beyond the Grave

Cedric Kanana
with
Benjamin Fischer

Foreword by Archbishop Onesphore Rwaje

PEMBROKE STREET PRESS

PEMBROKE STREET PRESS

Dying in Islam, Rising in Christ: Encountering Jesus Beyond the Grave
Copyright © 2018 by Cedric Kanana and Benjamin Fischer

All rights reserved. First edition 2018.

Requests for information should be addressed to:
Pembroke Street Press, LLC, 307 S State St., Nampa, ID 83686

English-language translations of the Qur'an are from Interpretations of the Meanings of The Noble Quran. Translated by Muhammad Taqi-ud-Din Al-Hilali and Muhammad Muhsin Khan. English edition. Dar-us-Salaam Publications, 1999.

All Scripture Quotations are from the English Standard Version. Copyright © 2001 by Crossway, a publishing ministry of Good News Publishers. Used by permission. All rights reserved.

All rights reserved. No part of this book may be reproduced, stored in a retrieval system, or transmitted in any form or by any means—electronic, mechanical, photocopy, recording, or otherwise—without written permission of the publisher, except for brief quotations in printed reviews.

ISBN 978-0-999-29041-5 (softcover)

Cover design: Amy Gilles

Printed in the United States of America

THIS BOOK IS DEDICATED TO OUR FAMILIES

Dorcus and Ebenezer
Brooke, Ruthanne, Laurelai, and Moriah
Kanyinya Parish
Christ the Redeemer Anglican Church
Diocese of Kigali
Diocese of the Rocky Mountains
Province of the Anglican Church of Rwanda
Anglican Church of North America
GAFCON

And the Everlasting Kingdom of Christ Jesus, the Lord and Savior

CONTENTS

Foreword 11
Acknowledgments 13

Prologue 19

1. Family Bonds 23
2. Things Fall Apart 29
3. A New Kind of Life 34
4. False Comforts 40
5. New Territory 46
6. Unholy Alliance 50
7. Recklessness 55
8. Vengeance 58
9. Osama 63
10. Another Path 69
11. "He who digs a pit…" 76
12. Jesus in the Mosque 84
13. The Undiscovered Country 89
14. A New Lease 95
15. Immigrant Education 101
16. Sanctified in the Truth 110
17. Backlash 114
18. Jesus is Stronger 120
19. Welcoming the Stranger 126
20. Turning Their Hearts Back Again 134

Epilogue 141

Glossary 147

FOREWORD

GLOBAL CHRISTIANITY IS CHANGING. For decades now, anyone who is conscious of the global Church has noted the dramatic spread of Christianity in Africa, Asia, and Latin America, along with a steady decline of faithful church participation in Europe and North America. Social scientists and scholars of religion have been pointing to population shifts, changing values, and economic causes. Noting the charismatic and evangelical nature of the growing portions of the Church, many of these observers have feared and lamented a revival of what they view as primitive, fundamentalist Christianity. But we in Africa think there is another way to understand what is happening in the global Church. For those who believe in the Sovereign God, we have to acknowledge that the Lord Jesus is the Ruler, King, Chief Shepherd, and Vinedresser of his people, and he is involved in pruning and growing his vine. God himself is changing his Church.

The story of my brother, Rev. Cedric Kanana, powerfully illustrates what God is doing in the regions of the world commonly called the Global South. More and more often, we hear accounts of the Lord calling people out of Islam or traditional religion through stunning means. We have heard of Jesus appearing in mosques to call the worshipers to follow him. We have heard of him speaking to crowds with a voice that thunders and shatters windows. He has literally written in light upon walls to convey his gospel. And all across the Global South, he is using his faithful people to speak and work in power — healing the sick, driving out demons, and reconciling mortal enemies.

Dying in Islam, Rising in Christ

Rev. Cedric's story is distinctive in that it combines all of these marvelous works of God. At a time when he was "dead in trespasses and sins, following the course of this world, following the prince of the power of the air," God made him alive with Christ and raised him from the dead — both spiritually and physically (Eph. 2:1, 5-6). Through a series of powerful acts, which you will read about in these pages, the Lord Jesus Christ has clearly chosen Cedric Kanana as a servant and evangelist to many groups of people, from Muslims and pagans to idle and unfaithful Christians. Hundreds of people have committed to following Jesus through Cedric's testimony and preaching, and it is my hope that this book will also be a tool for many others to place their trust in the Almighty God.

I also hope that readers will notice how the Lord has guided Rev. Cedric to remain within the structures of the Church as he labors in his ministry. At a time when the fertile spiritual soil of East Africa lures many promising young leaders to strike out on their own and create isolated churches without accountability, Rev. Cedric has consistently demonstrated the humble spirit of Christ, submitting to authority and strengthening the Church instead of dividing her. It has been my pleasure to know and encourage this young man in his evangelistic ministry, and I hope and expect his story will continue to inspire faith and open many eyes to the glory of the Lord Jesus Christ.

– *Most Rev. Dr. Onesphore Rwaje*
  Archbishop of the Anglican Church of Rwanda
  and Bishop of Gasabo Diocese

ACKNOWLEDGMENTS

WE OWE THE EXISTENCE OF THIS BOOK to the orchestrating work of the Lord Jesus, who arranged our unexpected meeting in the home of our mutual friend Elson Mageza while we were each visiting Byumba, Rwanda, from abroad. The Lord's instruments on that occasion prominently included Bishop Emmanuel Ngendahayo, official host for both of our visits and our friend and brother. He and the Diocese of Byumba likewise made possible and fully supported the three-month residence in Rwanda of the whole Fischer family, during which the initial transcriptions of the story were made. For that stay, we are grateful for Ben's sabbatical from Northwest Nazarene University and from Christ the Redeemer Anglican Church in Nampa, Idaho, both of which financially and spiritually supported the venture. Jake Lee ably cared for Christ the Redeemer during the absence. In Rwanda, Dan and Kari Hanlon (with Josiah and Nora) refreshed us, but especially the Fischer family, by providing a loving and quiet sanctuary in their home. During the writing of the book, the Diocese of Kigali and Bishop Louis Muvunyi have consistently supported and encouraged the project. The Parish of Kanyinya has often graciously been without their pastor for his evangelistic ministry. Eric Fristad, and Ted and Becki Carrico read and commented on the manuscript, helpfully shaping its tone. Vaughan Roberts, Bishop Ken Ross, Dave Abels, Bill and Ann Fischer, Blair Carlson, and Bishop Thad Barnum were crucial encouragers for the book to come to publication. In many ways, Jonathan Fristad was the doctor for this book, checking in on its progress and then delivering it into the world. It would not exist without him.

Beyond the composition of the book, other acknowledgments are necessary. I, Cedric, greatly thank the Lord God Almighty who has been faithful to me all these years. I also thank my wife Dorcus for her prayers and encouragement, as well as our son Ebenezer for blessing us both. I thank God for Rev. Ben Fischer for the work done for this book. May God bless all his efforts. Thanks to Blair Carlson, Bishop Emmanuel Ngendahayo, and Robert Berry, each of whom played an inspirational role and provided theological training. I thank my church leadership who mentored me and received me the way I was; God used them to shape who I am today. I also thank all Bishops of the Province of the Anglican Church of Rwanda, especially my own Bishop Louis Muvunyi in Kigali Diocese, along with my colleagues in the diocesan staff and fellow pastors.

For my part, I, Ben, want to praise God for his sustaining grace. Helping to bring this story to print has been among the most unexpected privileges of my life, but also one of the most humbling. I am still awed that I was given the task to record it, and I thank my brother Rev. Cedric Kanana for trusting me. Along with those mentioned above, I must joyfully acknowledge my wife Brooke and our daughters Ruthanne, Laurelai, and Moriah. They are uniquely part of the story, still living it, and the most significant voices speaking life into the book's creation.

MAP OF RWANDA

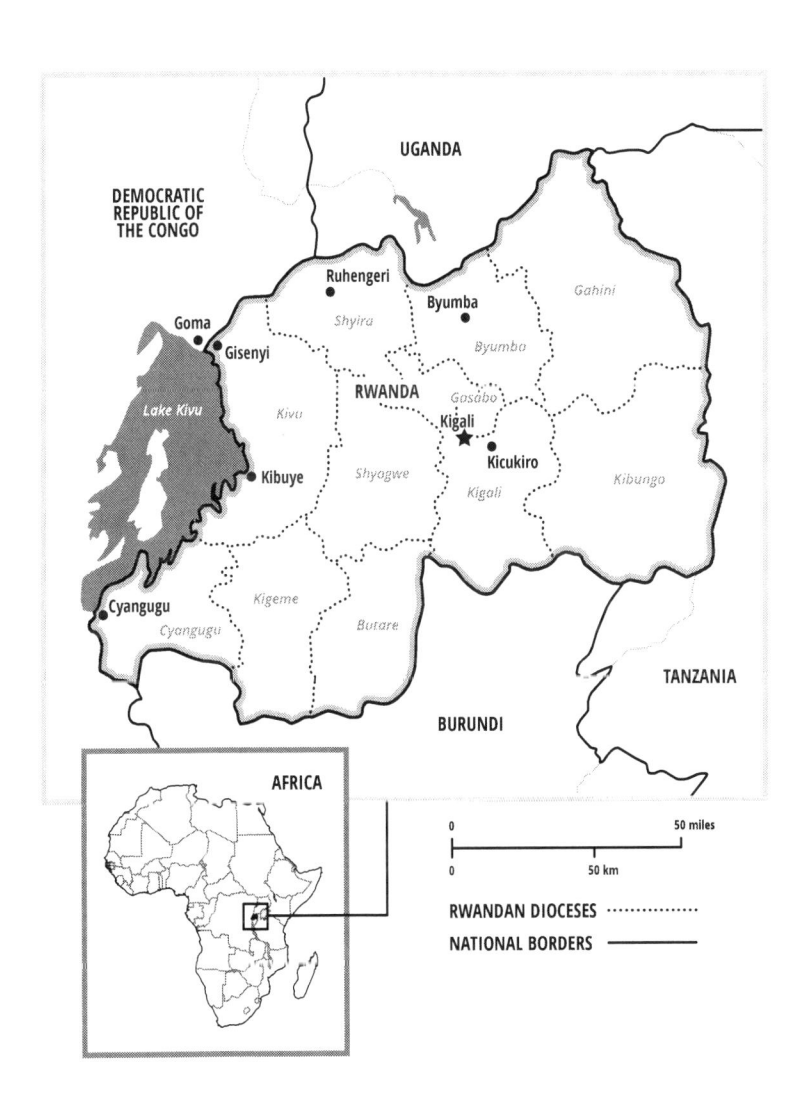

PROLOGUE

WITH THE SOUND OF THE DRUMS pounding in the distance, I quickly picked my way between the terraces of growing maize and sweet potatoes, looking for the shortest path up the hill. The warm morning sun shone full on my face as I repeatedly glanced up the hill towards my goal, the church on the hilltop. With bare feet kicking up the red Rwandan dust, I hastened like I had an appointment to keep, but I had no idea what would await me when I arrived. How could I? A Muslim imam does not typically rush to enter Christian churches.

The deep, regular rhythm of the pounding drum thundered out the call to worship every Sunday morning at 9:30am, announcing that the Christians would soon begin their singing and prayers. It wouldn't be long before the call and response of their song would mark the moment when their leaders would gather outside the building and walk together into the church, carrying high their cross and banners. Their song, "Tukutendereza Yesu," would echo down the hillsides, welcoming their people to the praise of Jesus and at the same time provoking the irritation of my people, the Muslims of Gisenyi.

As my legs churned, every few minutes I became suddenly aware of the fact that I was almost naked—wearing only a loin cloth—but the summons of the drum and the vivid memory of his face kept me rushing along. I was climbing the hill in obedience to his irresistible command. Just a short time ago — a little over a half hour earlier — my body had been lying lifeless on a table, washed and prepared for burial. And now the One who had brought me back was compelling me to respond to this call of the drum.

A collage of repeating mental images kept time with the patterned crops. My feet rushed past the deep, dark vines of the tightly clustered yams. I saw his feet, bare beneath the gleaming white robe. Then the vibrant green of maize, with outstretched fronds. I saw again his uplifted hand, gesturing towards me, revealing a hole in his palm. The starry purple and white flowers winking amongst the rich green of the Irish potato plants. There again was his face, steady and calm. His eyes fixed on me. What was the expression? Commanding, serious, smiling, all mingled together. Even as I ran I felt the flush of fear and embarrassment combined with comfort and delight. The drum continued to roll out its upward summons, and in the steady beat I could hear his commanding voice, "Remember."

Halfway up the hill, I heard the drum joined with voices, "We praise you Jesus, Jesus Lamb of God." It was their song, the song of their Revival, reminding them of their beginning eighty-five years ago.

I quickened my pace, striving up the steep course. "We praise you Jesus." Yes, I was going to praise Jesus. I laughed out loud at the irony! The imam running naked to praise the God of his enemies. But I had seen Jesus. And I had seen my real enemies. I had felt the icy clutch of their taloned grip. Whatever any human might do to me, whatever meanness or cruelty they might wish me — Muslim, Christian, or pagan — I would never again mistake them for the real enemies and their master, the Enemy of my soul.

And the song rose higher, "Jesus Lamb of God, Your blood cleanses me." What did it mean? The Lamb and the blood? I thought of the blood of sacrifices — the goats and bulls brought to the African gods to turn away their anger or win their favor. The priest or priestess would hold one horn of the victim, and taking the hand of the one bringing the sacrifice, would place it on the head of the animal. And then the knife to the animal's throat, and the blood. "Jesus Lamb of God, Your blood cleanses me," they sang. It must be sacrifice. But how does it cleanse? And could it cleanse me?

At last I rounded the ascent and came to the hilltop. By the open doors of the Anglican church, a young girl pounded on a massive calfskin drum. Her eyes were closed and she sang with the others, whose voices now poured from inside the clay-brick building. "Your blood cleanses me, I praise you, Savior."

Whatever else might be, this I understood: I praise you, Savior. I had been dead, and now I was alive. Hands of darkness had bound me and claimed me, and I had been powerless to prevent them in any way. I had been marked for destruction. And then he had come. His presence alone had scattered the evil and destroyed every sign of them. He had saved me. He had sent me back. I would praise him as long as I lived. There was one sure fact in the world: Jesus is the Savior.

As I walked towards the door of the church, the girl at the drum opened her eyes. She dropped the sticks and ran screaming into the church, as if she had seen a ghost. Naked to the eyes of the world, an imam proclaiming Jesus, I followed her through the open doors.

Chapter One

FAMILY BONDS

THE WEEK I WAS BORN, my parents hosted one of the largest birth celebrations that our village near Gisenyi, Rwanda, could remember. Hundreds of guests — family, friends, and members of the Muslim community — travelled from all over the Lake Kivu region for a four-cow feast. The sheikh had finally had a son, and his shame was taken away.

For five years my parents had hoped desperately for a son. Although they had two daughters, in Islamic culture it is considered a matter of shame to have only girls. So after the second girl, they started to feel pressure from the Islamic community, as well as scrutiny from all the village and family. It did not matter that my father was the sheikh of the Muslims in our district, nor that he had been one of the first converts to Islam in Rwanda, back in 1964. Regardless of the country in which the community resides, Islam is an honor-shame culture. Living with ongoing shame is connected in the community's mind with some secret cause for divine displeasure, and no one, regardless of status, was immune from marks of shame like a family of only daughters. For five years, the embarrassment and the shame had mounted, even while my parents took more and more extreme measures to ensure that they would have a son.

From the local perspective, my parents had an impressive array of resources to try to address their lack of a son. They were the wealthiest family in the district since my father was the manager of a factory, and my mother brought in considerable income through her services of witchcraft. She was the priestess of her clan's god, Biheko, which made her a master of African traditional religion and its many forms of magic and witchcraft. By providing incantations, charms, formulas for blessings and curses, and rituals for sacrifice, she earned both money and influence in the community. So to their problem of a male child, they brought all their perceived resources of power. With my mother acting as priestess, they went to sacred places bringing cow after cow to sacrifice to Biheko in order to gain blessings of fertility. Biheko was supposed to be especially protective for our clan but was also thought to have particular influence on reproduction and the fertility of the land. To supplement these sacrifices to Biheko, my mother added incantations and potions, charms and totems, all aimed at controlling and manipulating the unseen powers of the world.

To add another magical influence from a different angle, my father would regularly take pages of the Qur'an containing *surahs* of blessing, grind them into a powder, mix the powder with water, and then bathe in these now-magical waters. These waters were supposed to convey the power of the scriptural blessings to the bather.

As the years passed without my mother conceiving, my father began to contemplate divorce to marry another woman who would produce a boy. Perhaps she was the problem, he reasoned. Perhaps she had personally offended Allah or Biheko. Growing more desperate, my mother went to consult the gods of other clans. One of these priests asked five cows for a single sacrifice.

It may be a surprise for some to hear of this mingling of Islam and African traditional religion. But in most of the world where Islam has a significant presence, Islamic culture contains this same blurring with Animism. Commonly called "Folk Islam," it accounts for between 70 and 85 percent of Muslims worldwide according to various estimates.[1] While "Formal Islam" focuses on the legal restraints, formal traditions of the Qur'an and Hadith, and issues of institutionalizing the faith, Folk Islam is concerned with everyday problems. To combat enemies, deal with discomfort, obtain success and material prosperity, Muslims resort to traditional spiritual practices that preceded the arrival of Islam and have re-

---

1. Rick Love, *Muslims, Magic, and the Kingdom of God: Church Planting among Folk Muslims* (William Carey Library, 2003), 21. Phil Parshall, *Bridges to Islam: a Christian Perspective on Folk Islam* (IVP, 2007), 16. Don McCurry, *The Gospel and Islam* (Missions Advanced Research and Communication Center, 1980).

mained side by side with it, in some countries for centuries. These very typical Folk Muslims will argue emotionally for the truth of the Qur'an, the honor of Muhammad, and the Seven Pillars of Islam, and then resort to magic and witchcraft when they feel threatened by others or need some kind of advantage. For example, countless women in African Islamic culture secretly treat their husbands to a love potion designed to retain their fidelity; the charm is meant to give the wife power over her husband's erotic impulses.

In the minds of these Muslims, who comprise the vast majority of East African Muslims, their syncretism of traditional religion and Islam is perfectly faithful to Islamic tradition. Indeed, belief in *jinn*, or spirits, is one of the Six Articles of Faith for Muslims, and the *jinn* are as much subject to external manipulation and control as humans are.[2] The Hadith (the name for the authoritative traditions of Muhammad and his companions) are full of magical practices, demonstrations of spiritualism, and attempts to control the *jinn* for the material benefit of the Muslim, or the harassment of his enemies. Similarly, the Islamic reverence for the Qur'an as a temporal deposit of heavenly power quickly turns it into a magical object, and Muslims use its words and phrases — sometimes literally cut out of the book — as tools to bring good or evil. My father's ritual bathing in the waters of Qur'anic blessings demonstrates only one of the ways the book is used for "contagious" or sympathetic magic.

Despite all their efforts at spiritual manipulations and appeasement of traditional African gods, when my mother did finally conceive, they acted the part of observant Muslims without any sense of duplicity and declared humbly that it was "the will of Allah."

The period of pregnancy was a tense one for my mother because my father made it clear that if another daughter were born, my mom would be sent away. She would carry the shame, but he would find a replacement. With such stress, it is a miracle in itself that she carried me to full term.

---

2. The Six Articles of Faith are (1) belief in Allah, (2) belief in *jinn*, (3) belief in the Holy Books of God, especially the Qur'an, (4) belief in the prophets of God, especially Muhammad, (5) belief in the Day of Judgment, and (6) belief in Allah's divine decree, or predestination.

Dying in Islam, Rising in Christ

When I was born on February 28, 1985, it was with tremendous relief that my parents sent out the welcome call for the celebration. In traditional Rwandan culture, children remain nameless before this ceremony, called *Kwita Izina*, about a month after the birth. Part of the hesitance is the high infant-mortality rate, bringing a reluctance to name a child before it is clear he or she will thrive. More importantly, though, is to involve the community in the naming process. Every child is not just part of a nuclear family, but also part of an outwardly radiating set of interlocking relationships: an extended family, a clan, and a village. Each of those forces—family, clan, and village—fix the child's identity. There should never be a time, it is thought, when a boy must wonder who he is. Since the child will be shaped by all these circles of belonging, its name must come through their input, too. On the appointed day, all the children of the village lined up, each one bringing a name. Some of them brought names of their own invention, others represented suggestions from their parents.

On either side of my parents sat the eldest sister of their respective families. Traditionally, their opinions would hold the greatest weight in this matter.

"Nizeyimana Asman Peace," said the first little girl. My paternal aunt grunted and wrote down one of the names. In modern Rwanda, it is common to combine a meaningful Rwandan name with a name from one of the families and a third Western or religious name, typically from either Christian or Islamic tradition.

"Swidiq Eugene," said a small boy in a Muslim cap. He glanced at my father from the corner of his eye. The maternal aunt latched on to one of the names.

"Nshumbusho David Abu-bakr," came the next boy. The paternal aunt, a Muslim, was pleased.

My eldest sister then stepped up. "Ndayisaba Kanana," she said, lifting one eyebrow in the direction of my father – a Rwandan equivalent of a wink. Both aunts pretended not to notice.

The next little girl stepped up. "Mukerarugendo John." My father frowned. "No Christian names," he said firmly and waved the child along.

And so it went on, with every child in the village offering a name. When all the suggestions were taken, the aunties and the parents conversed privately. According to Rwandan custom, the aunties choose the name. But among Rwandan Muslims, the father actually makes the choice.

It is something of a rhetorical dance as the aunties try to hit on what the father wants.

"See how strong he is. He will be like Abu-bakr, a warrior," said the paternal aunt, referring to the first caliph of Islam. She looked at my father, whose expression did not change as he looked at the squirming baby. Catching his hinted displeasure, she added, "Or perhaps Asman?"

Seeing the same response, the other aunt came to her rescue, "No, this one is long-awaited. I think Ndayisaba (which means, 'I ask God') Kanana." They both looked intently at my father, expectant. He raised his brows, indicating there was something he liked.

"But what does Kanana mean?" the other asked bluntly, breaking a bit from custom.

Playing her part well, my mother broke in, "It is like Canaan. The land of Promise for Abraham's people." This interjection was their confirmation.

"Yes, I think one name should be Kanana," said her sister, with the other aunt nodding.

They had it now. The maternal aunt had seen the other hint. They glanced at each other and she smiled reassuringly. It would be her prize.

"I think Swidiq Kanana," and that settled it.

So my father named me Swidiq Kanana, a name meant to establish a destiny for me in the Muslim community. After so much longing and waiting and expectation, his own identity in the community would be poured into mine. Not only was my father the local sheikh, but he had provided the land and financed the building of the mosque in our district. With his own hands he had helped to lay the bricks, each one a symbol for him of laying the foundation for Islam in Rwanda. In naming me Swidiq, "trustworthy one" or "one in whom trust is placed," he thought to sow into my future the role of leadership of the mosque he had built and of the Islamic community in Kivu he had helped to establish.

He aimed to defend this high destiny with fierceness. Even as relatives and neighbors came to see the long-awaited baby boy, my father would not allow anyone to touch me who was not a Muslim. In his mind, I would be a pure Muslim, untainted by any Christian infection or influence. With assumptions shared by Muslims everywhere, he spoke Arabic words of the Qur'an over me as I lay swaddled in my mother's arms. These words were meant to be words of blessing, power, and protection, and they were meant to bind me to the Muslim community with spiritual cords.

The story of my life is in many ways the outworking of these sincere attempts to bless, which instead brought curses. It is the story of the unbinding of these cords, the breaking of the bonds that bound me and my family to a kingdom of darkness. It is the story of One who came personally, in great mercy and grace, to release a captive and add a soldier to his mighty Kingdom. And it is a story of restoration and reconciliation beyond all hopes of possibility.

Chapter Two

THINGS FALL APART

AS A CHILD SO LONG EXPECTED by my parents, my earliest years until about 8 years old were marked by comfort. Truth be told, I was a bit spoiled. To our family of five, another sister and a brother were added. With so much energy, worry, and resources invested towards my birth, my parents sheltered me from any cause for anxiety. I had no idea that the lives of my family were seriously threatened in those years.

Prior to the late nineteenth century, when the European colonial powers scrambled for areas of Africa to claim as their colonial possessions, Rwanda had been a united kingdom. With a single language, Kinyarwanda, and shared customs across the country, many clans had come together under the Mwami, the king, understanding themselves to be the Rwandan people. Three ancient people groups, representing three waves of migration into the region, mingled and intermarried. The Ba-twa, a pygmy people who lived mostly in the forests, were the earliest of the three. Then came the Hutu, who had always prized the cultivation of the land. Lastly, but still anciently, the Tutsi had come, bringing a love for cattle-keeping and a knack for administration. It was under Tutsi leadership that the clans had been united and organized as a kingdom, and for several hundred years Rwanda was the most stable kingdom of East Africa. Clan united with clan through marriage alliances, and families could shift between Hutu and Tutsi according to the number of cows they owned and the local social position they held. When Germans and Belgians made excursions into East Africa in the 1880s, the kingdom of Rwanda accepted German advisors to its court with the provision that governance would remain in Rwandan hands.

At the conclusion of World War I, the distant powers of Europe determined that Belgium would have control of the Rwandan kingdom and the people of Burundi to the south. With slow and steady influence, the Belgians imposed the European notion of fixed racial categories on the intermingled people of Rwanda. Incorporating the German fascination with race, the Belgians identified individual people as Tutsi, Hutu, or Twa depending on physical appearance, disregarding the centuries of mixing and movement between the groups. They issued ethnic identity cards and, giving favoritism to the minority Tutsi whom they thought more like Europeans in appearance (identified as lighter skinned, taller, with long and narrow noses), they alienated the great majority of the country. In this separation and favoritism, the Belgian imperialists sowed the seeds of hostility and revolt.

When Rwanda gained its independence in 1961, the Hutu majority reacted with the pent-up anger of decades. Mirroring a pattern all over Africa, wherever European colonial administrations had organized the native population along invented lines, they left a heritage of division and civil war. From 1961 until the Genocide against the Tutsis in 1994, a civil war burned slowly in Rwanda, in many and terrible ways trying to establish the stability of the tragically lost pre-colonial era.

Although my father's family had been identified as Hutu, my mother's family clan were culturally Tutsi and prided themselves on carefully maintaining their clan's traditions. They were cattle-keepers, observant of traditional religion, and wary preservers of tribal customs handed down for generations. In 1986, the whole family was endangered as there was a brief but aggressive move against Tutsis in the region. Tutsi exiles who had joined the National Resistance Army in Uganda aided in the overthrow of the Ugandan dictator Milton Obote. Rwanda's President Juvenal Habyarimana took the opportunity to enforce a policy prohibiting any exiled Tutsis from returning to Rwanda. In the rural communities across Rwanda, the President's move against the minority group was seen as an official sanction for persecution, thereby spurring local violence as significant numbers of Tutsis were killed without repercussions.

During recurrent periods like this, my mother and her children were all in danger. But my father's heritage and position in the community proved to be a shield to us in those years. Not only as a sheikh but also through his position as an influential voice in the ruling party of the local government, Dad was able to keep his family guarded from these persecutions.

But in 1994, no one of Tutsi lineage was safe. As the ongoing Civil War between the Hutu-controlled government and Tutsi rebel groups had reached a stale-mate, President Habyarimana accepted the reality of power-sharing through the Arusha Accords in August of 1993. Grievously, the Hutu Power movement was unwilling to take the path of peace. Hutu Power refers to the movement of racialized, ethnically conscious Hutus who had determined that Rwanda would only have peace as a nation of Hutus only; they were in many ways the Rwandan sapling produced by the same ideologies and spirits of evil that gave rise to Nazism. Since 1991, they had begun to organize local Hutu militias in Kigali and the larger towns, openly training for violence against their Tutsi neighbors. When Habyarimana's plane was shot down on the 6th of April, 1994, the *Interahamwe* militias (meaning "those who attack together") began the planned work of exterminating the Tutsis and their sympathizers around the country.

Initially, my father tried to protect the family by bribing his friends and colleagues in the local government. But before long, our family was hunted. As a male with a Hutu father, I and my younger brother were at first considered safe, while my mother and sisters were in constant danger. But as the genocidal ambition of the violence became clearer, so did the scrutiny of any with Tutsi heritage. Hostile people in the village began remarking that I was too much like my mother. I had soft hands like a cattle-keeper — wealthy and spoiled — not the calloused hands of a field laborer. These were tell-tale markers used to divide those who were killed from those who did the killing. So despite my Hutu father, I too was marked for death. For the first several weeks of intense killing, Dad hid us from place to place, along with other members of my mother's family. But it was clear we had to escape the country. Through his connections, he found a way to pay for our protected passage to Goma in Congo, where many refugees were gathering.

Dying in Islam, Rising in Christ

When the Rwandan Patriotic Front (RPF) — the predominantly Tutsi army invading from Uganda — succeeded at ending the genocide after 100 days and securing the country, we quickly received communication from my mother's brothers that we should return immediately. These uncles were in the RPF and were able to facilitate our safe return, just as refugee camps in Congo began to be infiltrated by members of the *Interahamwe* who had fled from the RPF advance. What had been safe havens turned suddenly into death camps. In the tense militarized atmosphere of mid- 1994, we returned to Gisenyi. But the family situation was not a restoration of our pre-genocide circumstances. As it did to every family and every village in Rwanda, the genocide desecrated everything it had touched.

Despite my father's successful efforts to save his wife and children, along with members of my mother's extended family, my uncles in the RPF had become bitter through the war and wanted no family connections to a Hutu. Her family's tendency to keep their tribal customs and lineage purely Tutsi now found a target in my father. They saw to it that he was imprisoned with Hutus who had participated in the genocide. Even further, they tried to force their sister to divorce her husband and marry a Tutsi man. Yet, my mother had seen the loyalty of her husband through deeply trying circumstances, and she had always appreciated that even when they were unable to conceive, he had not enacted his Quranic privilege as a Muslim man to marry other wives. So she resisted her brothers' efforts, even to the extent that she threatened suicide if they carried out their plans to have Dad killed in prison. When they saw that she was immovable, they relented and allowed his release.

But the damage was done. Dad had risked his life and every available resource to ensure Mom's safety and to secure the rescue of many from her tribe. As he sat in the overcrowded prison, suffering from deprivation and beatings, he thought over the pains he had taken. He stared at the hard, dirt floor for hours on end, growing more and more bitter and angry. He remembered the money he had paid as Hutu militants demanded that he turn over his wife and children. He recalled standing at the door and claiming we had fled, even while we and my cousins were huddled on the roof. He had saved so many, and now they had betrayed him. The bitter root took hold and grew in the dark loneliness of his imprisonment.

When he was suddenly released through my uncles' reluctant intervention, he ignored my mother's pleas that she had tried everything to save him from her brothers. He changed the locks on our house and refused to let my mother collect even basic belongings. Overnight, we became homeless. And just like my mother's family had attempted to force a new marriage on her, his family arranged for a new Hutu wife. At 9 years old, my home and family were broken.

For us, as for the whole of the country, the horrible betrayals of the genocide had ripped the fabric of interconnection that bound families and villages together. Not only was trust unthinkable, identities were in disarray. Family, clan, and village were all colored by the genocide in some way, and while everyone knew that the tribal identities had been central to the destruction, most people did not know where else to turn. For Muslims, though, who on the whole resisted participation in the killings and often protected fleeing Tutsis, the Islamic identity provided a refuge. Not only then, but in the years since, Rwandan Muslims have been rightly proud of their role during the genocide, and it has been a source of attraction for many who became disillusioned with tribalism or family heritage. The claim of having clean hands partly explains the large increase in Rwanda's Muslim population since the genocide. Nevertheless, as our situation demonstrates, there is no such thing as equality in Islam.

Not only did Islamic tradition offer no protection to my mother and her children, on the contrary, the Quran and Hadith gave explicit support for my father's abandonment. In Islam, a woman is considered a slave to her husband, and a man may do with a slave whatever he desires. According to *sharia*, or Islamic law, a man may divorce his wife simply by saying his wife's name and *"taliq"* ("is divorced") three times. To our Muslim community, he was seen as entirely within his rights, and she alone bore the shame of the rejection.[3]

---

3. For detailed discussion of the status of women in Islam and in *sharia* law, see Ergun Mehmet Caner and Emir Fethi Caner, Chapter 8, "Women: Love, Marriage, and Property," in *Unveiling Islam: An Insider's Look at Muslim Life and Beliefs* (Kregel Publications, 2009), 132-41.

Chapter Three

A NEW KIND OF LIFE

WHEN MY MOTHER WAS EJECTED FROM MY FATHER'S HOUSE and a new wife was brought in to take her place, all five of us children went with her. But there was nowhere for us to go. The genocide had destroyed or scattered my mother's family across East Africa, and for many years afterward they were fearful to return to Gisenyi and the scenes of their trauma. We took shelter with some compassionate neighbors for a brief time, crammed into whatever spaces they could spare. Before long, though, my mother was able to get a small, three-room mud-brick house where the six of us crowded to sleep. Carrying the shame of being rejected by her husband, my mother had no standing in the Mosque, and the Muslim community was unwilling to give her any help.

I could see the terrible weight on my mother, as she scrounged for food and worked for pennies digging and harvesting other peoples' land. Her religious services as a priestess of Biheko had been for her own tribe, and their dispersion meant that her reliable source of livelihood was dissolved. So as she sought means to feed us, I increasingly felt the reality that each mouth was a burden. A few times a week I would go back to my father's house around a mealtime, even just to relieve my mother for that brief moment.

A New Kind of Life

On one of these occasions, Dad's new wife came in to find me in the sitting room — the sparsely furnished front room of every Rwandan house. She had immediately developed a hostility to everything connected to my mother, and although I was the only one of the children permitted to visit their house, she never made an effort to hide her disdain. Finding me there at mealtime, her disgust boiled over.

"What is this thief doing here?" she said. "All he does is take. He only stays alive so he can steal."

I crumpled where I sat, having nothing to respond. While the words stung and brought tears to my eyes, the worse pain was that my father stood by silent as I cried. There was no care or comfort in him. Rather than step in and offer some other way for me to see myself, he let her words strike home. I, who had once been his hope and treasure, had somehow been transformed in his eyes. To him, I had become accursed.

When I left the house soon after, I truly believed that I had been cursed by this woman's words. With my father's tacit consent, I had received her wicked words into my heart and allowed them to redefine me. Had anyone seen me walk the twisted path home that night, they would have seen a frail boy struggling to take each step. The dirt itself seemed to weigh down my feet, and the tearing pain inside worked its way from my heart to my mind, bringing darkness.

That night I lay curled in my small sleeping space on the floor. I thought of suicide. As I considered how it might be done, my thoughts led quickly to death for Allah. Perhaps in that way, I could both end my life and gain something for Islam. I had heard of terrorist groups who recruited and trained even young boys to wage war against infidels. Perhaps I could make my way to places where they were fighting and could carry a bomb. But even while I weighed these possibilities, they felt empty. Suicide would fail to accomplish what had begun to grow in my mind: punishing my Dad. If he did not care about me, then my death wouldn't bring him the pain I wanted to inflict.

Eventually, the dark words of my step-mother worked their way into prominence. I am a thief, she had said. I am alive only to steal. This notion settled in as the truth — I am a useless thief. And if a thief, I must join the other useless thieves. That night I decided to find boys who live on the street, and the next day I went to join them.

Situated just above the equator, Rwanda sees the dawn every day of the year at 6am, and the whole country gets moving not long after. Early the next morning, I woke with the rest of the town and shuffled towards the main market area of Gisenyi and my new life. With numerous entrances, the market covers a massive block at the center of town. Like markets all over Africa, rows upon rows of thickly packed tables and stalls create narrow passages teeming with people of all ages, searching through brilliantly colorful cloth, sheets, and rugs. Other areas hold piles of used clothes and shoes, sacks, buckets, tools, and plastic goods from China. Ripe fruits and vegetables, rice, beans, and potatoes – the Rwandan staples – fill the central area with vibrant color, while the pungent odors of butchered meat and freshly caught fish waft throughout. The whole scene resembles an East African fabric, seemingly disordered bursts of bright color held together by distinct dark lines, which somehow suggest patterns of repetition—an ordered disorder.

Just outside the main entrance, I found a group of dirty, rough looking kids trying to flip coins into a can. They saw me watching them from a safe distance, and three of them sidled over to see why I was lingering alone.

An older teenage boy asked, "What do you want? Why are you watching us?"

"I… I don't have a home anymore," I said, trying not to sound too afraid. "I need to live on the street."

"You don't know anything, do you?" the older boy said. "You can't just walk up and say you want to live with us. You're a weakling. Why would we want you?"

I didn't know what to say. I couldn't think of any reason why anyone would want me. And then the words of my step-mother came back to me. "I'm a thief," I found myself saying.

"Alright, baby thief, we'll see," he said, and then he pushed me to the ground with a hard shove in the chest. The other boys jumped on and gave me a beating. My tender little body absorbed the shocks of knees and bony fists. With bruises and a bloody face, I passed through the first phase of my initiation, confused by the senselessness of what they were doing.

That night I lay on a pile of rags in a narrow alley between two shops. I realized I had been spoiled. I had not been prepared for this life, and I didn't know how I could bear it. I wanted to be with my mother, even hungry and jammed into the tiny house. But as the tears slid silently down my cheeks, I told myself I couldn't go back. I could not be a burden to them, and this was the life I was destined for.

The next morning two of the older boys took me to the center of the market. They told me to act like I was looking at the repaired shoes — I was obviously in need of a new pair. They stood beside me, like older brothers, occasionally pointing out a pair. But while they played this charade, they kept glancing around for something. Then one of them pulled me up.

"See that lady over there, the one with the red bag on her wrist?" he said. I nodded.

"You go grab that bag and run down the aisle that way," he said, gesturing along a particular exit. "Her hands are full, so she can't hold on to it. When you're out, run back to the alley. We'll meet you there." He gave me a little shove towards the lady.

I meandered slowly toward the lady, hesitating. When I looked back over my shoulder, the boys were gone. I debated with myself about whether to keep going, but the words kept echoing, "He's only alive to steal. He's only alive to steal." This was the life I was meant to live.

I shuffled my way past the lady, then turned suddenly and grabbed the bag with a jerk, and just as they had said, she dropped everything so I was able to run. As I ran down the aisle towards one of the market entryways, I could hear voices crying out, "Thief! Stop! Thief!" I shot out of the entry — right into the arms of a guard. The boys had directed me exactly to the place where I would be caught.

For the next five days, I huddled in a cell with other minors, choking on the stench of our waste. Periodically, the guards came in and knocked us around, giving us hardly anything to keep us alive. There were too many thieves to keep in jail for a long time, so the policy to discourage crime was to give kids a miserable taste of punishment. In those five days, I came to understand a prime principle of street life. No matter how bad it was on the street, it was better than in jail.

When I was released, the gang of boys was there, waiting. They knew exactly how long I would be jailed. They surrounded me with a few slaps on the back. We went that afternoon to an alley, and the oldest boy, the leader of this gang, took out a bag with small rolled papers. He put a rolled paper between his lips, struck a match and lit the paper.

As he held it out to me with two fingers, he said, "Swidiq, living here you're going to need this. We live like animals. Outside. Dirty and cold. It's the worst life, and we have too many problems. This stuff will make you forget your problems."

My first experience with marijuana was horrible. My weak, 9-year old body had a strong negative reaction. Not only did I vomit, but I was delusional, and my mind was so overwhelmed that I thought it would explode. Thoughts, sounds, and racing images threw me into a blur. I held my head in my hands, but I could not escape what I had put inside me.

Nevertheless, it was the beginning of a regular ritual. It was how we got by. When the misery of our life became too much, when the cold or the disgust or the loneliness became too much to bear, marijuana promised an escape. And I learned to run there for comfort.

I later learned that my step-mother laughed victoriously when she heard I had gone to the streets. She was heard bragging about the effect of her "medicine" and her curses. Some readers may not immediately understand what I mean here. Just as my mother was a priestess of her tribe's god and practiced ritual magic, my step-mother was also a practitioner of witchcraft and the manipulation of spirits. Although she was not known for her sorcery across a wide region or connected to a particular god, she might be called a village witch, able to produce potent charms, especially curses and charms for enemies, and "love" potions for women to control their husbands. Some of her secret activity was once made very public when she visited a Christian gathering with a friend. At the time to begin the meeting, a man was simply praying an opening prayer, and she fell down in convulsions without apparent consciousness. Then she began shouting out confessions of her witchcraft, of burying charms and "medicines" in various peoples' house enclosures.

This kind of evil spiritualism can produce profound effects on those outside the kingdom of Jesus Christ. But spiritual manipulations can also affect Christians who have not understood their identity in Christ. Professing Christians who do not see themselves as truly forgiven and under the blood of Jesus, or who have willfully walked apart from the Lord's ways, open themselves to the power of evil. If we are not looking to the power of Jesus for salvation and strength, we are looking to our own power, and the power of one human is not stronger than evil.

In other words, it was true that the spiritual manipulations of my step-mother had an effect on me. I had no greater power to whom I could appeal, and I even accepted her curses as the truth. The more I lived into the lies about my identity and my future, the more authority I gave them in my life. In a way, to accept the lies as truth was to submit myself to the forces of evil as having legitimate authority over me. And as these forces desire the destruction of all human beings, they were bent on my destruction as well.

Chapter Four

FALSE COMFORTS

FOR FOUR YEARS I WENT BACK AND FORTH from the streets to my mother's home. When it seemed like survival at home was getting too tough for the family, I stayed with the boys on the streets. But in seasons when home life could handle me without too much trial, I stayed with my mom and siblings. Through those years, I slipped deeper and deeper into the bondage of habitual marijuana smoking and the world where drugs are worshiped.

In one period when crops were bad and life seemed especially tenuous at home, I looked for some way to help my mother and sisters in their suffering. I had learned from the older boys on the street that the dealers in marijuana would use kids to smuggle the drugs across the border with Congo, the source for most of the marijuana used in East Africa. Marijuana could be grown throughout the jungles of Congo without any hindrance from governmental authorities. So the Rwandan sellers would send kids between the age of 12 and 15 over the border to Goma, where the growers would deliver the finished crop and package it for sale. The kids would then re-cross the border without suspicion. Through the older boys in the gang, I offered my services to the dealers in Gisenyi, and at 12 years old I took my first smuggling trip to Congo.

Following the directions of the dealers, I had no trouble linking up with the marijuana suppliers. On the Congolese side, individual selling units of the dried leaves were put together as "packets," and on this first trip I was charged with purchasing 100 packets. When the packets were bound together, all 100 were only about the size of a hardback book. I easily made the purchase and started to make my way back towards the border. As I picked my way through the crowded streets, an idea dawned on me: maybe I could fool everyone.

By the time I boarded the mini-bus for the Rwandan border, I had stopped off in a shop to pick up an item for my plan. Before reaching the border, I got off the bus and ducked behind a building. I was wearing a *thobe*, the long robe worn by Muslim males over the top of loose trousers. Under this robe, I took out my purchase, a long piece of fabric worn by East African women, called a *kitenge*, and wrapped it around my waist. This *kitenge* created a pocket where I concealed the package of marijuana. I was carrying a bag, like someone who was visiting friends or relatives, and the dealers were expecting that I would pack the drugs at the bottom of the bag inside some clothes.

As I came to the border, I made sure to approach a station where there were several Rwandan border guards. Rwandans authorities always staff official posts with several guards in order to ensure accountability, but I chose a station where there was an extra guard who would be free to chat. Passing through the station and the routine bag check, I put on all my charm and chatted with them like a little brother. After passing through, I lingered inside the border area talking with the additional guard. These crossing areas are called "Petit Barriers," or small borders, because they primarily serve foot traffic, and once you pass through the barrier, you can be seen from any vantage point near the barrier. I was counting on the marijuana dealers seeing this ongoing conversation with the guard. Out of the corner of my eye, I could see two of them watching me — one was especially conspicuous for being too thin, with a head too large for his frame. He was the one who had given me instructions.

Passing out of the Petit Barrier area, the two dealers waited for me to move out of sight from the guards. Then they quickly caught up with me, having worried expressions.

"What happened?" the thin one asked. "Why were you with the guard?" the other quickly added.

"They found the pack when they searched the bag," I said.

"No! What did you tell them?" the thin one asked anxiously.

"They let me go. They said I was too young to arrest, but they took the marijuana," I said.

"But what did you tell them? They know you're working for someone," the other said.

"I didn't tell them anything. They asked who sent me. I told them it was boys I didn't know who promised to give me 2,000RWF." At this, the guys seemed relieved but also anxious, looking all around, making sure nobody had followed me.

"You're sure you didn't say our names," said the thin one.

"No, they believed me," I said.

"Okay. Sorry, kid, we can't use you anymore. They'll watch you every time now. They'll follow you. We can't be seen talking to you." With that they hurried away, still glancing here and there.

I headed towards my mother's home feeling pleased with myself. I had easily fooled both the guards and the dealers. I had traveled only about five miles, but the world had just gotten much bigger. There was a rush of self-satisfaction as I felt for the first time in my life something like a sense of power. I realized that I could outsmart people. I could play a role. I could use my charm and get what I want. Yes, I thought, I am a thief. This is who I am, and it is exciting and powerful. And now I had resources.

With those hundred packets of marijuana, I began my own business of selling. Because I knew where those dealers operated, I was careful to test out new areas and find new buyers. There were other groups of street kids, other busy market areas, and plenty of people filled with despair ready for me to exploit. The horrors of the genocide and its resulting trauma had left countless people desperate to escape their memories. Along with Rwanda's longstanding problem with banana beer, drug use was on the rise. Young and old alike were willing to try anything to ease the pain, and I was there to help.

With some extra money turning up in our house through my selling, my mother decided it was time to send me to school. I joined Primary 4 (P4), the equivalent of American fourth grade, at the age of 12—thoroughly addicted to marijuana and eager to sell to other Primary School students.

I was assisted in my efforts by the teacher in charge of discipline. When he first saw me, I caught his attention not simply because I was a 12-year old in a class full of 9 and 10-year olds; he knew he was looking at a marijuana smoker. One day early in the term, he casually asked, "So where do get your stuff?"

"What stuff?" I said, pretending ignorance.

"You know what I mean," he said. "The stuff that makes life a little happier." He put two fingers to his lips when he said this, pantomiming a smoke.

For a moment, I wasn't sure how to respond. I stared at the ground. Was he trying to trick me into admitting it so he could throw me out of the school, or did he want some drugs himself? When I stole a glance at his face, I saw the answer. He had a glint in his eye and the slightest twist of a smile played at the corner of his mouth. And on his lower lip I caught sight of the revealing crease that always gives away a regular smoker. I lifted my head and gave back a sly smile.

In exchange for one pack of marijuana each day, the Discipline Teacher gave me free rein to sell and dispense to whomever was interested inside the school. Within two years, well over half of the boys in the upper grades of my primary school had become regular marijuana smokers.

It was during this time that I became closer friends with a boy named Faraji. I had known him through the Gisenyi Muslim community since we were very young, but during the genocide and those three years of my drifting in and out of living on the street, we had not spent much time together. In the school, he became my ally in everything. When I would go over the border to Goma, Faraji came along to double the capacity. Two Muslim boys in their long robes looked perfectly natural crossing the border. Even today, but especially in the unsettled periods when refugee flight resulted in many separated families, it was normal to have aunts and uncles living on both sides of the Rwanda-Congo border. Faraji and I maintained our story of making regular visits to family, and each time we came back from Goma, we were laden with packets of marijuana.

The fear of mutual destruction tied us tightly together and kept us honest towards each other, so Faraji and I were fast friends by the time we were 14 years old. I was in P6, or sixth grade, when we went to see a martial arts film. Although I don't remember the title, it was a Jackie Chan movie about revenge. In the film, Chan's character sees his kungfu master killed by a villain, and fueled with the desire for revenge, he trains intensely on his own and grows skilled and powerful in kungfu. The climax of the movie is a confrontation with his master's killer. Even as I was watching the film, I felt my emotions stirring an internal rage. I saw an analogy in the anger of Chan's character towards his master's killer and what I was feeling towards my father. Hadn't he almost killed my mother by his rejection and hadn't he left us desperately scratching for our lives? When the moment of vengeance came in the film, I was thirsty for it. In seeing Chan's character find satisfaction in destroying his enemy, I seemed to taste it too. I wanted that satisfaction in its fullness.

As Faraji and I left the cinema, I began to turn over a plan in my mind. I would be like the character in the film. I would find someone to train me in kungfu, and when I was strong enough to confront my father, I would use it to kill him.

That week, Faraji and I found a kungfu school in Gisenyi. During the next year, I moved rapidly through the introductory level belts. My anger motivated me with focus and drive, giving me the ambition to move as quickly as possible to the levels where real harm can be learned. When I finished Primary School the following year, I had already come to the green belt, which was the third of seven levels towards kungfu mastery in our school.

More importantly for the larger course of my life, I had found a new source of comfort: the thought of destroying my father. As I trained, I imagined the shame I would put him through. I cherished the thought of crippling him, leaving him begging for his life before I finally took it from him, as he had taken my happiness from me. This thought of revenge guided my plans and fueled my training.

In my conscious thoughts, vengeance more and more took shape as a picture of myself as powerful. No longer the frail street boy at the mercy of the older boys, I saw myself dictating to others and demanding submission. So the desire for vengeance and the dream of personal power worked their way into my inmost self, mingling with the bitterness of rejection and fear. And like those poisons, they settled well with who I believed myself to be. I was among the worthless with nothing to lose, but like the thief I was, I could take what I wanted and somehow make life bearable.

False Comforts

Through these adolescent and early teenage years, I was still a fixture in the Muslim community of Gisenyi. Whenever I was with other Muslims, I would join them in performing the *salaat*, the five daily prayers of Islam. On Fridays, I attended the mosque that my father had built and joined with the other Muslim males in midday *jumu'ah* prayers, which is the Muslim Sabbath time of prayer. But at all these gatherings, I went through the motions without any knowledge of what our recitations meant. The Arabic words poured from my mouth, my body bent and bowed, but my eyes were glancing around the room, looking for something I might steal. Especially, I sought to steal from my father. Although I visited his home only rarely, those occasions served to stir my bitterness and rage, and every little theft felt like I was doing justice.

Chapter Five

NEW TERRITORY

PRIMARY SCHOOL IN RWANDA ends at P6, when students all over the country take a national examination that determines the type of secondary school (or high school) each student can attend. Those who perform poorly or whose family have little financial resources will attend the local government-run schools. Sometimes these schools are built and maintained by the Catholic or Anglican Churches, but the teachers and curriculum are provided and paid by the government. In the past, the curriculum and the teaching in these government schools were in French, but at the start of 2009, the whole country dramatically switched to education in English. In either case, the problem remained — curriculum is presented in a second language, sometimes a language only minimally understood by the teachers themselves. So the pay is low, the teachers are often poorly motivated, the students tend to be uninterested, and the whole atmosphere hovers on the edge of futility. If a student scores high enough on the national exam, and if the family can possibly afford it, they will avoid the government schools.

The better schools are private and follow a boarding school model inherited from colonial days. Sprinkled throughout the country with varying degrees of tuition and strictness of discipline, they sometimes adopt the government curriculum, sometimes not. While more recently the best private schools have connections with overseas partners, traditionally the top schools were run by various societies and missions of the Roman

Catholic Church. As a former Belgian colonial possession, Rwanda has many Catholic schools that were founded during the colonial era, which gives them a reputation for dependability. Most of them have maintained a connection with the Catholic mission society of their founding. They tend to have nice campuses and access to more global resources, and like the reputation of Catholic schools in America and Europe, they are known for strict discipline. And just as in the colonial era, most of them are boarding schools. Due to the quality, only students who score well on the national exams (or whose parents have deep pockets) have the opportunity to attend these schools.

To everyone's surprise, including my own, I passed the national examinations with high marks. I had given only about one day each week to study and homework, and I had used the time between and after classes to sell marijuana. Evenings and weekends I gave to martial arts training or trips to Goma to fill up my drug supply. All the while, my own use of marijuana had continued steadily, and each day was highlighted by my time of comfort with smoking. Nevertheless, somehow there I was with an opportunity to attend one of the best schools in the country.

As I had grown in confidence and began to bring in money for the family through my drug sales, I had become the leader of our household. My mother, three sisters, and younger brother all looked to me for support. Because of the burden I felt to provide for them, I decided to stay close to home and attend a nearby Roman Catholic boarding school called Ecole D'Art de Nyundo (in English, Nyundo School of the Arts).

The first term began in early February. On the night before I left for school, I packed my bags slowly. Like anyone before a significant change, this move into the boarding school gave me pause. Moving back and forth between home and living on the streets had become normal, and I had learned a distinct boundary: just don't get caught. Even though the school was only a few miles from home, a boarding school seemed like a whole different world, with different boundaries than I had known. I was a little scared. In a moment of painful clarity, I wondered if I would make it in the school. Would I be able to manage my addiction? Would I find a place to smoke undetected? If I couldn't use it, would I even be able to think clearly enough to learn anything? I worried about the shame of failure. I already knew that if I went very long without smoking, my body — especially my brain — started to protest with pain. A few days before, I had taken a quick trip to Congo to purchase a supply of marijuana for my own use — 40 packets of marijuana cut for cigarettes. With anxiety about the future swirling around, I stowed the marijuana carefully.

The next day I walked into my new home, the dormitory for boys. It was a long brick building comprised of a series of rooms, each with a single outside door opening to a covered walk. There were between eighteen and twenty-four beds in each of the rooms. Each boy's private space consisted of a single shelf and half of the space under the bed.

The first night was hard. I had not gone for an entire day without marijuana for three years, and I found myself wide awake through the first half of the night. Every sound seemed magnified. A cow lowed at a house just beyond the school wall. The night was so still that I could hear it moving in the stall. The steady breathing of the other boys in their deep sleep became irritating to my nerves, seeming almost to penetrate to my bones. Somewhere in the distance a toddler woke from a nightmare and cried its desperate plea for rescue. I smacked a mosquito whining by my cheek.

Finally, in the middle of the night, I cautiously slid my sheet off and stood up. When I was sure no one else was stirring, I stepped into my sandals and went quietly out the door. I went straight to the toilets and smoked my joint, settling my brain into its comfortable state. Now relieved, I made use of the moonlight. Working in the shadows of the buildings, I canvased the school, looking for spots where I could smoke without arousing suspicions. I stayed out of sight of the main entrance and the guard house, and checked into spaces that would be part of my routine. At the end of the row of bath stalls (each one a 3' x 4' mud-brick space big enough for a bucket and a naked boy), I found a ruined stall where the roof had fallen in. Nobody would be using it or thinking to check inside. This would be the place.

Over the next two weeks, I returned each morning to the ruined bathing room. While the other boys were bathing, I smoked my joint of marijuana, and when most of the others had gone, I quickly bathed. Within a few days, I began looking for other smokers. Marijuana smokers seem to have a special ability to identify one another, but there are also signs I knew to look for. I noticed when someone had dry lips, blood-shot eyes, and droopy eyelids. I looked for the jittery walk and noted when someone tended to laugh too easily. But most tellingly, I had an eye for the dent in the lower lip of someone who would often withdraw from others. By the end of those first two weeks, I had identified all the smokers in the school and began to sell to them. Most helpfully for these insidious purposes, I found a customer in the Prefect, a retired army officer whose job was to ensure discipline in the Boys Dormitory. It seems like this irony is often repeated in developing regions, so that a lack of established accountability structures allows for failings in those who are in positions of trust. Like a wall with holes and breaches, there are many easy openings for the clever and unscrupulous looking to exploit the situation.

I was becoming just such a wary opportunist. When my 40 packets of marijuana were all used or sold, I called Faraji and we took a quick trip to Goma, now confident in a steady market inside my school. With full knowledge of the Prefect, I would be free to come and go whenever I needed to resupply. The thought occurred to me that in reality, I would be the real Prefect of the dormitory. He belonged to me. I was the one in charge.

Chapter Six

UNHOLY ALLIANCE

THE GROUP OF MARIJUANA SMOKERS IN THE SCHOOL naturally became attached to me through their dependence on what I was providing them. When a drug seller maintains a steady supply at a cheap rate, there is a twisted loyalty that develops between the drug user and his supplier. Within the first academic term, however, I sought to deepen the nature of this loyalty. I had gained a taste for power through lying, stealing, practicing kungfu, and controlling others through drug dependence, and I wanted more of it.

Everyone follows models for life in one way or another. Without a positive connection to my father or other men in my family, one of the catalysts for a way to see myself came from a story we read in our Literature class, which was a French-language telling of the *Epic of the Kingdom of Sundiata* from Mali and Ghana.[4] In this legend, the ancient hero of the Muslims in West Africa, named Sundiata, unites the Muslims of the region in an ongoing war against the kingdom of Ghana led by the sorcerer king, Soumaoro. Through the use of sorcery and magical items, Soumaoro and his warrior son, Sosso Balla, are untouchable – able to change shape,

---

4. The version we read was a French edition *Soundjata ou Epoque Mandiginue* by Djibril Tamsir Niana, first published in 1960. For an English translation of Niana's text, see *Sundiata: an Epic of Old Mali*, D.T. Niane (Pearson, 2006).

Unholy Alliance

are invulnerable to weapons, and can transport themselves safely out of battle. With the help of evil jinn, they were invincible. Although the legend ends with the triumph of the Muslim hero Sundiata over the sorcerers' army, Soumaoro and Sossa Balla remain shadowy figures — with armies defeated but personally indomitable. The sorcerer king Soumaoro disappears into a cave, while his warrior son Sossa Balla is somehow above punishment and has to be persuaded to join Sundiata's retinue. In this legend, I became fixated on the young warrior Sosso Balla.

As he was described in the legend, he had all the qualities that I had begun to appreciate. Not only did he have magical powers and personal access to the spirit world, he also had invictus — the unconquerable will. Even the victorious hero Sundiata had to acknowledge Sossa Balla's right of self-determination; if Allah had determined that Sossa Balla could not be the ruler, still he could not be ruled. I imagined myself like him. Although I was subjected to conditions and circumstances beyond my control, I was unconquerable. I too would defy authority and create my own path.

With this inflated vision of myself in mind, I started giving little demonstrations of martial arts to the boys in the school. By this time I had earned the blue belt, the fifth of seven levels towards mastery, and was growing physically stronger. More and more, other boys were drawn to me, especially the boys already dependent on me for their marijuana habit. Following the view of life I had absorbed from the street gang, I formed a group of these boys into a kind of gang within the dormitory. In order to be part of this group, boys had to take marijuana and submit to Islam. We called the group Sosso Balla. Like the namesake from the *Epic of Sundiata*, we saw ourselves as powerfully untouchable, outside the school's structures of authority.

When we first began to separate as a distinct group, our real knowledge of Islam was admittedly small. The few of us who had grown up Muslims of course knew the basic Arabic phrases for the *salaat*, but we hadn't been taught anything of the Hadith or how to understand the Qur'an. Still, there was an added thrill to our exclusivism in uniting defiance of school rules with proselytizing for Islam within the Catholic school. Everything we did was a mockery of the school's authority. By the conclusion of Senior 1, my first year in the Catholic school, we had become a noticeable presence.

Dying in Islam, Rising in Christ

Before the start of Senior 2, Faraji and I took a longer trip to Goma. Along with resupplying marijuana for the first term, we went to learn Rasta dancing. Rasta dancing had come to Africa from Jamaica as part of Rastafarianism, a mingling of Roman Catholic Christian practices, pagan spiritualism, political pan-Africanism (the notion that something intrinsic unites all Africans), and a devotion to marijuana experiences. The religion itself hasn't made much headway in Africa because pan-Africanism seems foolish to Africans, who are very conscious of their national and tribal distinctives. But mostly emptied of the religious aspect, Rasta dancing has spread throughout sub-Saharan Africa. In the late 1990s, its popularity was surging. Rasta entrepreneurs would organize events called "Boom," where they would set up a stage and some kind of perimeter in a public place or school ground, and charge a minimal fee to enter. With loud music inviting huge crowds of young people, experienced dancers would lead the crowds in learning dance steps to popular American music, especially Michael Jackson.

On our many short visits to Goma, Faraji and I had seen these Boom events from outside. We had decided to learn as best we could and come back to Rwanda with our own business plan. Within a week, bouncing around between different events, we became proficient enough to teach others the basic dances that were most popular. Along with our supply of marijuana, we had something else to import across the border to Gisenyi.

When the term started and my Senior 2 year began, I was ready to capitalize on the Rasta craze. My school sometimes organized weekend activities for students' amusement, especially during the long stretches when the boarding students were away from family. With all the members of Sosso Balla pushing to influence the scheduling of these weekend activities, I soon had the chance to put on a Boom event in the school. Following the format Faraji and I had seen in Goma, we set up a stage, borrowed speakers, and played Michael Jackson. After a little demonstration, I taught students the basic steps. The attention and enthusiasm of the crowd was intoxicating, and the more they seemed to have fun, the more energetic I became. By the end of the first Boom, they were jokingly calling me Little Jackson.

With some practice, almost anyone can learn to dance, but not everyone can lead a crowd into the fun of it. Faraji was never really interested in being front and center, but with him taking care of the music, I found a new thrill and a new sort of power in these Rasta events. I could dance, but more importantly, I could pull a crowd together and usher in an experience. Through a few visitors to our school events, word began to spread to other schools and I received invitations to host Boom events all around the Kivu region. It was through these events that I came to Kigali, the capital, for the first time. Before long, almost every weekend I was traveling somewhere as Little Jackson, with long dreadlocks and hefty supply of marijuana, to lead a Rasta Boom.

It was also at this time, as a 16-year old, that Islam took on a more significant place in my life. I had consistently shown up to *jumu'ah* prayer whenever possible, and I had formed Sosso Balla as an exclusively Muslim group, but up to this point the practice had been perfunctory. We performed the *salaat* as our class schedule allowed, but the practice was more for demonstrative defiance than anything spiritual. But the power I was experiencing through leading the Sosso Balla group, and the ability I found to captivate an audience with Rasta, combined at this time with a desire for spiritual vitality. Since I was leading boys into Islam, I figured that I should have more to give them and know how to lead them farther.

I started to dedicate Saturday mornings to memorizing the Qur'an. In this pursuit, my distant father was very glad to support me and provided whatever learning aids I asked for. The Qur'an can be divided into seven equal parts, each one called a *manzil*. By the time I had memorized the first *manzil*, my zeal to convert others to Islam had grown. Since Sosso Balla was a Muslim group, I aimed to make more boys want to be part of us or at least associated with us. Rasta dance, martial arts, and marijuana all served as temptations to draw others, with the single proviso that if a boy wanted to keep associating with us he had to convert to Islam. Like most East African Muslims, the meaning of the Qur'an or the significance of Hadith traditions was less important than memorizing Qur'anic verses and practicing recitation. Just as sorcery and witchcraft co-exist with daily prayers for most Folk Muslims, I also found no contradiction in merging this new zeal for Islam with drug and alcohol use, defiance of authority, and personal aggrandizement. Not unlike the West African Muslim hero, King Sundiata himself, any means were acceptable for the end of bringing about conversions to Islam. The only thing that mattered was the confession of the faith.

Dying in Islam, Rising in Christ

In this strategy I was following the example of my Muslim elders and of typical Muslim practice through the ages. In regions where Islam is in the minority, it has generally been the practice for Muslims to use all sorts of material persuasion and bargaining to gain adherents. Particularly in regions with high poverty, including East Africa today, Muslims will build a small mosque along a roadside where there are few or even no Muslims. Typically funded from foreign sources of wealth, regional leaders will use these mosques as bases to offer food and clothing to the impoverished in the local villages. After initially receiving gifts, continued support will be upon condition of conversion — after which the giving usually stops. Likewise, where a Muslim owns a local business, he typically offers jobs only to Muslims or those who will convert to Islam. In this way, the empty mosque is slowly filled, and the impoverished converts who were at first happy to find help and support come to find themselves trapped in a religion that will not allow them to leave. Christians may feel a twinge of shame to recognize similarities between Muslim proselytizing and tactics of evangelism that Christians have sometimes used. Wherever Christian evangelism competes with Muslim efforts to convert, it is well for Christians to be clear about why they love and care for their neighbors, and to bring to the forefront the glorious truth that grace is freely given.

Chapter Seven

RECKLESSNESS

THE EXPERIENCE OF POWER AND CONTROL of others had so shaped my view of myself that nothing seemed beyond my reach if only I stretched out to seize it. Depending on the circumstances, I could charm and deceive, or if need be, manipulate and intimidate. From time with the street kids, I had learned to hide my own weaknesses while looking for them in others, and I had discovered the kinds of desires that motivate people. Yet underneath this inflated self-narrative there remained the deep-seated sense of ultimate worthlessness. It was a dangerous combination, more and more producing a recklessness that disregarded any thought of consequences.

To aid my martial arts, I started working harder at strength training. I bought a set of dumbbells, and whenever I was not in class, I was pushing myself to get stronger. I worked up to jogging around the school grounds carrying 20lb dumbbells. I knew I was becoming an object of concern for the school authorities, which only added to the pleasure of it. Out of the corner of my eye, I could see the gate guards watching me as I jogged past. And the Prefect, my regular marijuana customer, made extraordinary efforts to be somewhere else whenever he knew I was conducting drug business or breaking other rules.

Towards the end of S3, my defiant posture took on a more reckless course. One afternoon period, I was bored with a class and was staring up at the ceiling when the voice of the teacher became more and more irritating to me. Suddenly, I stood up and walked towards the door. The teacher, a small and usually timid man, shouted, "Swidiq, go back to your seat!"

I stopped and turned slowly. I fixed a steady stare on him without speaking. His eyes opened a little wider behind his wire spectacles. He said again, but with a slight quiver in the voice, "Go back to your seat or there will be consequences."

I continued to look steadily, and with perfect confidence and a hint of laughter, said, "No. And you know you'd better not say anything else about consequences." When I walked out, he was silent. The class sat stunned. We all knew this teacher would not risk a beating, and from that point, I had free rein. When the mood struck me, I absented myself from class, preferring to sleep or smoke.

Not long after, with my defiance growing to new heights, I went out on a weekend binge with Faraji. I took a supply of marijuana, and we met up with some friends who were soldiers in the army. Sitting around with them in drugged hilarity, looking at their guns, I thought about what I would do if I had one. In a moment, my father's face leapt to mind. How quick and easy to make an end of him, I thought. When Faraji and I left, still unsteady, I told him I would need his help one day to kill my father.

With this thought of murder flickering in my mind, I walked straight toward the Main Gate holding a cigarette in one hand and a beer bottle in the other. I was almost within the gate when I realized where I was and what was in my hands, but by that point, I no longer cared. I called out loudly to some friends, daring anyone in authority to challenge me. I saw the guard at the gate turn as if he were looking for something, pretending that he didn't see me.

But others saw. The Headmaster of School, who lived in a house within the school grounds, saw this brazen entrance and organized an emergency meeting to expel me. On Monday morning, when the whole school gathered for our regular Assembly, the Headmaster read a letter publicly announcing that Swidiq Kanana was officially expelled. I was called forward in front of the Assembly and given the letter. Before the Assembly was dismissed, I was required to leave. I took the letter without concern and nonchalantly headed towards the Main Gate. I immediately walked along the outside of the grounds and climbed back in through a hole in the fence that we often used for going in and out at night. I went back to the dormitory and slept all day.

When the boys returned to the dormitory after the late study period, about 9:30pm, I woke and went out. I walked straight to the Headmaster's house, which was on the school grounds, and pounded on his door.

The door opened, and he startled, "What are you…"

I cut him short, bringing a knife to his throat. I backed him inside and kicked the door closed behind me.

"What? What do you want? Do you want money?" he said, trembling with fear.

"You shut up and listen to me," I said. "You're going to reinstate me. Right now you're going to reinstate me or I'll kill you! I have nothing to lose. You have family and a life. I have nothing. I'll kill you. I promise I'll kill you, and even when they throw me in jail, I'll soon be released!"

"I… I can't. It was public. Everyone saw."

"I don't care. You're going to undo it. Write another letter. I don't care what anyone thinks." My mind was racing. I was not even sure what I was planning or how I expected it would work out. But he was trying to take my position away. He was trying to use his power over me, and I would not be controlled. I would not be made powerless again.

A thought raced into my head. "You've got some kids back there," I said fiercely. "I'll kill them. Reinstate me or I'll kill them now." To increase his fear, I nicked his neck enough to make him bleed.

"Okay, okay, I'll do it!" he said. "I can write a new letter. Just leave us alone."

With a hand gripping his shoulder, I stood behind him as he shakily wrote out a brief statement that Swidiq Kanana had fulfilled all that was required of him and was immediately reinstated. After I took the letter, he sat motionless with his head in his hands. As I went out the door, he had not moved.

There was no further attempt to get rid of me. It seems that the Headmaster and other school officials resigned themselves that after the National Examinations I would be gone. I was reinstated, and the school turned full energy to focus on the Exams. No doubt they expected, with good reason, that I would fail.

We took the Exams a few weeks later, and it was a great irony and miscarriage of justice that when the results came out, I had earned the top score in the Nyundo School of the Arts. Almost all the other boys in Sossa Balla had failed.

Chapter Eight

VENGEANCE

THERE IS AN EAST AFRICAN PROVERB, "He who owns calamity, eats it with his family." It means, more or less, that the trouble you invite is bound to affect those closest to you. However painful your family might be to you, they are part of you, and you of them. Particularly in the kind of village life that forms the foundation for African thinking, a man's issues are inherently the family's issues, even the whole clan's issues. In my mind, no matter how much my father wanted to be distanced from his children, we were the trouble he had brought into the world. He could not escape us forever. I was determined to make sure of it.

With the National Exams finished and school over, high school students all over Rwanda were home from November to the end of January, the equivalent of America's summer vacation. I was back at my mother's home in Gisenyi and back spending every day with Faraji. At the kungfu school, the masters saw my physical development, and after several weeks of trials, I was allowed to test for the black belt. When it was awarded, I knew I was ready for revenge.

I shared my plans with Faraji. Since that weekend binge with our friends in the army, I had been formulating how I could destroy my father. With Faraji's help, I would steal a gun from one of the soldiers. Then I would go to his house, and with Faraji keeping watch, I would confront my dad. I would use all seven bullets in the pistol, making him suffer as

Vengeance

I killed him. With each shot, I would shout what it was for. Two bullets for the legs that ran away with all the family's wealth and left us destitute, homeless, and begging. Two bullets for the hands that snatched and held all our belongings, even our clothes and my mother's magical items, which left us in rags and unable to help ourselves. And to finish him, there would be two bullets for his eyes that were blinded to his children and our desperation, leaving a final bullet for his forehead—one shot to answer all.

To cover the murder, our plan was to report a revenge killing from the time of the war. The period from 1998-2002 was a time of instability in Rwanda. Our western neighbor, formerly Zaire, had recently become the Democratic Republic of Congo in 1997. Although the Rwandan government had initially supported the coup, the new president failed in his promises to curb and extradite the Hutu Power militias who had escaped after the 1994 genocide. Rwandan military forces were supporting Congolese rebel groups who opposed the new government, and members of the old Hutu Power militias were taking advantage of the confusion and infiltrating Rwanda from Congo and Burundi. Particularly in the western provinces where we lived, they had recently made raids and set up ambushes, killing government or church leaders. Since my father was known to have helped his Tutsi wife and family during the genocide, and since he was a person of prominence and wealth, it was plausible that he would be targeted. My intended execution would not be hard to believe as coming from the militia fighters.

Faraji and I set a day, and we invited one of our friends who was a lieutenant in the army to spend his day off with us. He was a regular marijuana customer, and we offered to share joints and buy the liquor. In the back of a disreputable little shop that kept the alcohol coming, we spent the early afternoon smoking and drinking, continuing to push the liquor his way. When he had drunk so much that he passed out, I took his pistol, concealed it in my clothes, and we headed straight for my father's house.

In the golden light of the late afternoon, we walked with purpose to my father's house. Throughout Rwanda, the more money a family has, the more securely the house is walled. From ancient times, families would build enclosures, within which they would build individual huts for each wife and her children. The family animals were also kept securely inside. Even after colonial days, the decline of polygamy, and the beginning of urbanization, families have continued to enclose their homes and possessions in protective compounds. Those in complete poverty have no enclosure, but anyone who is able will construct some type of fence. These range from tightly grown plants, to bound stick-fences, to mud- and stick-wattled walls. But the wealthiest will construct tall brick walls, studded along the top with broken glass bottles embedded in the cement. Such was my father's house, brick-walled and secured by steel gates, and completely private. Once inside, I could attack him without observation or interference.

The hollow metallic thud of palm on steel startled me as I pounded on the gate. Faraji stood tensely next to me as we waited in silence. We could hear the scuff of approaching feet inside, and then the sharp ring of the key turning back the bolt in the lock. As the door swung open, my father's eyes blinked recognition for an instant and then flew wide open as I pulled out the gun and stepped forcefully towards him. He backed up quickly and silently, and Faraji closed the gate with a clang behind us.

"Into the house!" I said, sharp and quiet. Faraji stayed by the gate, watching and waiting in case anyone came in response to the disturbance.

When we entered the house and he turned towards me, the rage of years poured out and I kicked him with full force in the chest. He went sprawling, his Muslim *kufi* cap flying from his head. Lying on the floor, gasping for breath, he stared up at me with his eyes wide.

"What do you want? Why are doing this?" he said between gasps.

"You stupid old man, why do you think? What did you ever do for me but leave us begging in the streets!? You stood by with your evil wife doing nothing while we were starving and wearing rags. You're going to pay now! For everything." This was just what I had planned to say. But when the words, "You're going to pay now" came out of my mouth, the thought sprang to my mind, "Get some money."

"Give me money," I found myself saying with gritted teeth.

"I don't have anything here," he protested with a disgusting whine in his voice. "It's all in the bank, but you can get it — as much as you want. I have the bankbook."

"Get it. Fast!" I said. As he pulled himself up and stumbled to a drawer, I glanced out to check on Faraji. He was there, watching and listening. In no time now, I told myself, he is going to hear shots. I didn't have time to think through how I could get the money from the bank if I killed him.

Bent in pain, my father held out his bankbook with a shaking hand.

Vengeance

I wanted to spit on him and throw him back to the ground where he belonged. I snatched the book and flipped it open to see the balance.

Inside the cover is a security photo of the account holder, and beside that a photo and the name of the next of kin or joint account holder. Shocked, I read there "Swidiq Kanana" and saw one of my old school photos. This made no sense. Something immediately shifted inside. I felt a softening. "Can I kill him? He loves me," I thought. Maybe it was never him that was the problem. Many people had said that his second wife had bewitched him. Her curses had bound me, maybe my father was her victim, too.

Just as I was internally battling, the door opened and this same woman came into the room. At the sight of her face, all the anger I had felt towards my father, all the hate and murderous intent, shifted from him to her. She screamed as I quickly set the gun down and grabbed her. I lifted her, turned her upside down by the legs, and dropped her on her head. She fell heavily on the paved floor and began crying in a high-pitched whine, with blood coming from her split-open head. The sound of her crying irritated me horribly, like it was scratching my bones. I grabbed the gun and cocked it.

"Shut up, woman! Shut up!" I shouted. But her crying lifted to a terrified shriek. I pointed at her leg and shot. She screamed and continued crying. I cocked the gun again, ready to continue her execution.

Inside my head, I heard, as if coming from outside me, "If you do this, you have to kill them both. But if you forgive him, you have to forgive both. If you kill her, he will have to report you." So I decided. I would leave them.

I said, "I planned to kill you for all our suffering. But I've decided to forgive you. I'm giving you your lives. You ought to die, but I'm letting you live. I'm letting you! Don't forget that. But if I leave and you tell anyone, I'll come back and kill everyone, even your children." With that, I turned and left without another word. I tucked the gun into my clothes and met Faraji's questioning look with a nod to the gate. Once outside, we hastened to a path apart from the main road, not wanting to be seen in case someone had suspected where the shot came from.

"What happened?" he asked. "I heard her scream and there was only one shot. Did you kill him?"

"I was just about to, and then he showed me that I've always had access to his money. It was like he was saying he's bewitched. She has a charm or a potion that controls him, and he's been afraid to help us because of her," I said.

"So what was the shot?" he asked.

"The witch came in just when he was telling me about the money, so I beat her and then shot her in the leg. I wanted to kill her so bad. She kept screaming and crying, and I just wanted to shut her stupid mouth forever. But then I would've had to kill them both."

"Won't they tell? They'll have to say something about her leg," Faraji said. He was anxious. This was not as clean and secret as we had planned.

"It'll be alright," I said confidently. "I'm serious, they're scared. They know I'll come back and kill them and her kids if they tell. I warned them. But if they tell, we can go to Goma. It'll be fine. I promise."

I kept reassuring him that everything would be alright, and we were able to get the pistol back to the lieutenant's holster long before he roused.

And they did keep quiet. My father had seen and felt that I was dangerous and in earnest. People along the street and in the neighborhood talked about hearing a shot, but it was assumed to be part of the instability. My father said he has seen Hutu militia in the fields. They couldn't hide the wound, though. Their story was that she had cut it badly in the sugar cane fields. To prevent crop thieves, farmers set up sharp barriers around their fields. My step-mother had her own fields, and she claimed that she mis-stepped and fell on a sharpened stick, also injuring her head. It was plausible enough, and the Muslim neighbors wanted to believe the sheik. When anyone wants to believe something badly enough, they will.

So I felt that my desire for vengeance was satisfied, and somehow I was kept from murder. I had made them suffer, and she would continue to suffer from her wound and from fear of me. I knew and they knew that I had overcome them; I was stronger. It gratified my pride that now my father could see that I was unconquerable. Despite all that had happened, I was no longer the helpless little boy crying in his front room or getting beaten by the street kids. Somewhere, in an unformed thought that I never let come fully to consciousness, I hoped he would think that I am not worthless.

Chapter Nine

OSAMA

BECAUSE I HAD SCORED SO HIGHLY on the National Examinations at the end of Senior 3, the Rwandan government offered me a scholarship to study at one of the best Roman Catholic-run government schools in the country. Founded in the Belgian colonial period by the monastic Society of St. Francis de Sales (called the Salesians), École Technique Officielle, or Official Technical School (ETO) Kicukiro is in the Kicukiro suburb of Kigali. (In 2008, the school was closed as a Salesian institution and reopened by the Rwandan government as Kicukiro College of Technology.) The large campus was the base of operations for the Belgian UN troops in the days running up to the genocide. On the night of April 7 and the morning of April 8, 1994, over 2,000 Tutsis took shelter inside the school grounds. The Belgian evacuation of troops and all Western citizens on April 11, and the resulting abandonment to immediate death of the 2,000 Tutsis, is one of the more well-known episodes of Western complicity in the genocide.[5]

When I came to ETO, I knew the school's reputation. For the first time, part of me wanted to do well academically. Having twice surprised myself and everyone else with my examinations, I realized that I had an

---

[5]. These events are documented in the PBS Documentaries *Triumph of Evil* (1998), and *Ghosts of Rwanda* (2004) as well as forming the subject matter of the narrative film *Shooting Dogs* (called *Beyond the Gates* in the U.S.) (2005) (Directed by Michael Caton-Jones).

aptitude for gaining knowledge with minimal effort. I wondered how well I might perform if I actually put some real effort towards learning!

So for the first term at ETO, I kept my head down and was cautious. I went to class and followed the rules for the most part. The school grounds were extensive, including two forested areas on the southern and eastern sides, and in that first term I often went alone to the groves of eucalyptus. The trees were tall and mature, and their silvery leaves shimmered when even the slightest wind rustled through. In the heat of the afternoon, their shade was a place of refreshment, as the sunlight created darting patterns among the pale trunks. I loved to pace the forest and just sit against a tree.

But even in that peaceful grove, there was a simmering battle going on inside. I went to the forest so I could smoke marijuana without worrying about getting caught, but in the solitude I also recognized that this was a chance. The slate was clean. Not a soul in the school knew my family history. Nobody knew me as a homeless, worthless thief, or as a headstrong uncontrollable rebel. With my dreadlocks and swagger, I still looked the part of the Rasta artist, but that could be changed in a day. What could I become? I hadn't forgotten what every Muslim child knows, that in my first hours, when I was swaddled in my mother's arms, my father had spoken the familiar words, "*Ilaha illa Allah. Muhammad rasul Allah.*" (There is no god but Allah. Muhammad is the messenger of Allah.) And many times in my first year, I had been told, he would lift up and tell me my name: you are Swidiq Kanana — I will entrust you with the promise — his own explanation of my name's meaning. I knew there was a way of being Muslim that I had not tried because it brought me too close to my father and his control. I no longer wanted to kill him, but I didn't want him to exert his influence in my life again. But who could I be? Each time I came to the thought, there seemed to be a blank.

Typically, this question of creating a new identity never faces a Rwandan. We know who we are from a dozen angles. We belong to a family, to a clan, to a village. We live within a heritage. Faith, religious practice, God or gods are woven through it all. Being and belonging have not been at issue. But all the guides of my identity had been wrecked. In this post-genocide, transient, uprooted life I had fallen into, the steady stepping-stones were absent.

I came to a conclusion in the grove. It was at the end of the short dry season at the beginning of April, and we had a recess in school for the Week of Mourning, a week for remembering the genocide which began on April 7. During that week, I was walking among the eucalyptus on a bright day, taking in their sweet smell, when the scene shifted. Clouds were rolling in. The forest darkened in a moment, and instead of eucalyptus I thought I smelled something dead. With a touch of coldness, for the very first time the thought struck me that hundreds of Tutsis had tried to hide in this forest when the Belgians abandoned Don Bosco, and each one had been butchered.

In the middle of that thought, I heard someone say, "What's the point? It all ends in death."

And deep inside my heart grew hard. I left the grove having decided not to become, not to choose a path. Of course, my negation was itself a choice, as I was thrown back into the dark emptiness of self and the naked fallen cravings for pleasure and significance.

I soon began to gather others to smoke marijuana. By the end of the term, whatever ambition I had felt for school had completely dissolved into the ocean of pride and the pursuit of power that had ruled me and was soon to move to new levels.

During the brief holiday between terms, I went over to Goma and got 100 packets of marijuana that included the plants' seeds. I separated the leaves and seeds, taking the leaves to smoke and sell. But the seeds I kept aside, and when I returned to ETO, I found a shady spot in the school forest and planted them. From there, inside the school, I secured myself a steady crop and began selling outside the school as well as inside. The sense of being above any law and invincible, which had given an ethos to the Sosso Balla group, once again dominated my self-perception.

As I had done before, I began training other students in martial arts. Now with a black belt, my instruction had more legitimacy and was more intense. Within a very short time in the second term I had established a reputation in the school as a dangerous person and someone to be feared and respected.

During a weekend period of free time, I was selling marijuana in a bad part of Kigali. In a backstreet bar, I overheard another deal on cash terms way beyond anything I was doing. The buyer was smartly dressed in a suit that was obviously expensive, and the fact that he wore sunglasses indoors seemed to indicate he did not want to be easily identified. When the deal was done and the buyer had made his hasty exit, someone introduced the seller as "somebody you should get to know." I told him my name and asked what he was selling.

"So you're the guy growing right inside the school," he said, laughing. "Nice move. Saves hassle, huh. Just doesn't pay much, though."

"It's alright. Enough for me. I take care of my mom and sisters and brother. But what was that deal you just did? I thought I heard 70,000! And you handed him just a little packet," I said.

He leaned in and spoke a little quieter. "Ever tried cocaine? It's a different world from marijuana, and a little bit goes a long way. It's not a dull, floating high. It's like flying in the clouds. I have some guys who bring it from Kinshasa. You can tell from the guy who just left, we have a smaller, more elite group of buyers who are willing to pay many times what marijuana goes for. They all have a lot to lose, so they keep their mouths shut. If you're selling, there's more risks, but the cash is way better."

That was enough for me. We talked awhile longer and began to work out a business arrangement. If I would put up some cash collateral, just to show that I was invested, he would take a little risk on me. Within a few weeks, I was managing his deals, selling tiny packets of cocaine for between $75 and $150 each — a huge amount of money for a Rwandan. For each sale, I got 20% of the profit. Selling my own marijuana and the other guy's cocaine, there was more money than I ever imagined passing through my hands.

I was selling to wealthy, surprisingly important people. Even among them, the truth of the streets still held: people were desperate to dull the pain of life. They had found that their money and their comfortable houses could not fill their emptiness or chase the fears that haunted them. Just like the street boys from my childhood, these rich people turned to drugs for comfort. Even though I could see it in these others, I knew I was in the same prison. I also took cocaine when marijuana did not seem like enough. It could distort reality better and more immediately than any other lie I had yet taken in. Yes, it was a prison, but it was the only one I thought possible. The best thing for me, I believed, was to try to rule the prison.

Inside the school, I turned more and more forcefully towards a mentality of dominance. My recklessness returned in full intensity. In the dormitory, I claimed the end of the last building for myself and three of my friends who had made a conversion to Islam. The last four bunks we positioned in a square, blocking off the rest of the dormitory. We called it Baghdad, and other students referred to me as Osama, invoking the terrorist Osama bin Laden. As if I were beyond the reach of any punishment, I brazenly dealt marijuana inside the dormitory, and other students smoked it in Baghdad without fear of being caught. Our area of the dormitory was thought to be immune from the intervention of school authorities. In fact, teachers and administrators knew we were breaking rules, but they feared entering the dormitory in order to confirm any accusation. This confident defiance led to increasing evil. Students would pay me and my friends to use our area for sex. Boys from all the dormitories would bring their girlfriends there at night, and we would pull across a blanket for a small degree of privacy.

This kind of behavior led to further ruin for everyone involved. Girls whose view of themselves had become badly damaged were vulnerable for exploitation, and I was ready to use anyone to further my pride and control. Using girls from the school anywhere from age 14 to 18, I started an escort service with men outside the school. There were plenty of drug customers who were looking for other means of distraction, and the girls were looking for money. I would charge 20,000RWF (about $25); the girl would get 10,000 and I kept the other 10,000. My darkness had become like a swirling cloud, sweeping up all those who got too close. It didn't matter whether it was a desire for strength or skill with martial arts, or the temptation of drugs, or the lure of sex, or simply wanting to be noticed by an exclusive group, anyone who moved close to me and this group was swept up in evil. It seemed as if the darkness around me disabled others' ability to know right from wrong, and they just followed my lead.

The rule of this Osama in his pitiful Baghdad was short-lived. Such rampant evil and total defiance were bound to self-destruct. There is a Rwandan proverb, "When you turn your words into knives, you will cut your lips." Before the year was done, my evil came back upon me.

A younger sister of the Deputy Headmaster, or Prefect, had started associating with one of the other boys in Baghdad. He brought her to our dormitory at night, and we were just stepping out to give them their time when I saw the young Prefect walking quickly towards our building. Someone had told him about his sister, and he was following her to save her from this mistake. His care for his sister had overpowered his fears.

When he tried to enter, I stepped in the doorway and prevented him.

"This place belongs to me," I said firmly and flatly, as if we were not in the school grounds.

"My sister is in there. You can have your area, just let me get my sister and go," he replied.

"No. You can go. I'm in charge here. If she wants to be here, she can be here," I said.

The Prefect tried to push past me. I shoved him back, then kicked him across the face so that he fell. A few other students, blinded by their embrace of wickedness and somehow eager to prove themselves, jumped in and continued to kick and hit him. When they finally left him, he was scarcely moving.

Other students had heard the noise and came to see what had happened, including the Prefect's sister. She knelt down next to him, putting together what had happened and realizing her part in it. As a couple of students ran to get help, I knew my reign at ETO Kicukiro was over. The police would be called and I would be held accountable. So I went immediately into the dormitory, threw all my belongings in my bag, and left. The next day I made my way back home to Gisenyi.

Chapter Ten

ANOTHER PATH

POLICE ACTION IN RWANDA IS HIGHLY LOCALIZED, so my retreat to our far western province kept me out of jail, and ETO Kicukiro was a better, safer place for my departure. My family was, of course, surprised to see me. To one degree or another they accepted my story that I had some conflicts with the teachers, and the administration took their side and forced me to leave.

Since I had become convinced that it was my stepmother's witchcraft that had blinded my father to his children's past plight, we had started to rebuild a relationship, and I could meet with him without animosity. So we sat down to discuss my options.

"A man should walk the paths that lead to the journey's end. My son, you know that I have always seen you as my successor," he said with seriousness. "I named you Swidiq because you are the one in whom I hope to entrust the mosque and the leadership in Gisenyi. Allah has given you many gifts. You are bright—think of your test scores! You are strong. People follow you."

"I'm trying to be a good Muslim. I am still learning the Qur'an," I said. "I have the first two parts in my mind."

He grunted, lifting his brows in the Rwandan way of acknowledging my statement.

"I need more time. ETO kept me too busy to concentrate. Not even time for Friday prayers." He was of course ignorant of my marijuana and cocaine dealings.

Again he lifted his brows, and we sat silent. He seemed to be working up to something, chewing over the words before he let them out. "You know what we say, 'If you are building a house and a nail breaks, do you stop building, or do you change the nail?'"

Rwandan proverbs can be taken in many ways and usually mean more than one thing depending on the context. Rwandans use proverbs as a means of indirect communication. In some ways it's highly respectful because it shows that you think the other person can draw his own conclusion. Of course, I knew there was a particular conclusion my father was hoping I would draw. At the very least, he was indicating that he wanted to treat me with the dignity of an adult. I puzzled over what he was saying. After several minutes in the silence, I connected the dots from where he had begun the conversation.

"I could go to the Muslim school," I said at last.

This was the new nail he was thinking of. He was thinking of his two houses — his family and *Dar al-Islam*, the House of Islam.

Over the last several decades, Arab Muslim countries and organizations for spreading Islam have multiplied efforts to promote Arabic culture and language in sub-Saharan Africa, to grow the House of Islam in creative ways. A mix of political and economic conditions, including poverty, the collapse of Communism, and anti-Western posturing, have contributed to many African leaders seeking new alliances with wealthy Islamic countries and organizations. African countries with Muslim minorities like Uganda, Gabon, and Benin have become members of the Organization of the Islamic Conference (OIC), whose stated goals include Islamization of the African continent. One of the key objectives of the OIC is to make Islamic culture the basis of educational curricula at all levels. Some of the strategies mirror what has historically been a Christian missionary approach. They include financing the establishment of primary and secondary schools, funding departments in universities, setting up special study centers, and sponsoring institutes in western universities and in Africa for the study of Islam and Arabic language and culture. Aiding this effort, to the extent that Western pluralism influences the educational policies of sub-Saharan African countries, they unwittingly cooperate with strategic Islamization. This Western pluralism is the door that has opened in Rwanda through the policy of government cooperation with privately funded schools. Our Muslim school was such a place.

Another Path

In some ways, the school was just like any other school in Rwanda. As part of the agreement with the government and in keeping with the effort to spread Islam, there were non-Muslim students along with the majority Muslim students. We learned Geography, History, Sciences, Mathematics, French, and other courses following the typical curriculum and geared towards the National Examinations. But in addition to the typical elements, the Muslim school offered extracurricular studies of Qur'an-based Arabic, Hadith traditions (that is, the traditions gathered about the life of Muhammad and his first followers), and *Da'wah* (Muslim proselytizing or mission). These studies all intersected with the rhythms of life in the school. During the day, we heeded the *adhan* (the calls to prayer) from the mosque connected to the school. The class schedule was arranged so that class began after the mornings prayers, and then breaks between classes corresponded with the midday and afternoon prayers, allowing the Muslim students to join the Islamic Community for the prayers. It also put strong social pressure on non-Muslim students to conform to what the school community was doing. Conversion efforts were helped that conformity to community and authority is a Rwandan trait anyway.

Along with the shaping environment of the Muslim school, something in my father's notions captivated me and began to rework the way I was seeing myself. Since the day my stepmother cursed me with the identity of a thief, I had believed that was my path. But I had learned that my father looked at me differently. There was another identity older and more enduring than her curse that connected me to him and to the house he was building, literally and figuratively. He had built our mosque, and I was his son, a cornerstone of his house. Rather than using Islam as a feature of an identity, I started to accept that from birth, a path had been laid for me to take my father's place as a sheik, continuing his legacy. I had an identity to embrace and explore.

These considerations gave me new hope and new direction. They seemed to take up all the threads that had motivated me. I knew I was a leader and someone who could talk persuasively. I had no fear of crowds or public speaking. To be an imam and someday a sheik seemed to fit perfectly with the skills that had grown in me. So with the same zeal I had given to martial arts, rasta, and drugs, I poured myself into training for *da'wah*. I would be a true servant of Allah.

Dying in Islam, Rising in Christ

In East Africa, Islamic *da'wah* is carried on primarily through what we call *muhadhara*, open-air preaching and debate with the goal of winning converts. Preparation for *muhadhara* has two main aspects: knowing the Qur'an and the weaknesses of others' positions. Following from where I had begun a few years before, I set myself the task of committing the Qur'an to memory, but also understanding a bit more what it meant. These two frequently do not go together. If I were to be able to debate Christians, I needed more than the ability to recite; I would also need to have convincing answers from the Qur'an. So in learning *muhadhara*, we found the most useful passages for presenting an attractive Islam. Ready at hand were surahs that promise peace for followers of Islam or that command the giving of alms to the poor. A favorite was "Save yourself from Hell-fire even by giving half a date-fruit in charity" (2.498). In the same way, I also learned what traditions from the Hadith were most effective in showing Muhammad in a good light.

Along the way, we also discovered what was important to conceal. For example, it was necessary to conceal the many verses condoning violence, such as surah 2.191, "And kill them wherever you overtake them and expel them from wherever they have expelled you, and fitnah [sedition or persecution] is worse than killing." Likewise, we had to carefully guard the most respected hadith, such as collected by al-Bukhari, that showed jihad as Muhammad's glorious standard: "Allah's Apostle said, 'I have been ordered to fight the people till they say: "None has the right to be worshipped but Allah." And if they say so, pray like our prayers, face our Qibla and slaughter as we slaughter, then their blood and property will be sacred to us and we will not interfere with them except legally and their reckoning will be with Allah'" (1.8.387). Instead, we learned to emphasize the Qur'an's surah 2.256, "There shall be no compulsion in religion." Although it was an early revelation and superseded by many revelations condoning killing and enslavement for those refusing to convert to Islam, my opponents would not know that.

On the other side of training, I engaged with the Bible for the first time. Although the Qur'an explicitly acknowledges the *Injil*, or Gospel of Jesus communicated in the Bible, as divinely inspired, Muslims also view the biblical gospels as corrupted by human beings through changes to the message spoken by Jesus. Whereas Christians teach that God inspired the Bible through many authors over many centuries and brought the inspired works into a single collection, the Qur'an is said to exist as a complete whole simultaneously in heaven and on earth, dictated by the angel *Jibril* (Gabriel) from the heavenly book straight to Muhammad alone. I did not read the Bible, but I was taught how it was inferior (we believed) to the Qur'an.

To prepare for *muhadhara*, therefore, we also learned where many Christians are weak in understanding their own faith. Limited theological training for pastors, along with a speed of church growth unprecedented in history, has created an African church that is passionate, alive, and expansive but not very knowledgeable. Most Christians in East Africa have little comprehension of how the Old Testament and the New Testament relate to one another, or how to read biblical books according to their genre, or individual passages according to their context. One result is that African Christians tend to read all of the Bible in the same way, as prescribing behavior. While I also had no real notion of how the Bible fit together, or that the Old Testament constantly points to Jesus, I did learn that Christians often feel anxiety about how to reconcile different parts of the Bible. The result was that we could point to Old Testament verses that (I learned later) are fulfilled in Jesus, and we could argue that Muhammad was the fulfillment. For example, in Deuteronomy 18:18, God says to Moses, "I will raise up for them a prophet like you from among their fellow Israelites, and I will put my words in his mouth. He will tell them everything I command him." We argued that this was a prophecy of Muhammad. Similarly, we presented Jesus as Muhammad's forerunner, who announced the coming of the final and only universal prophet who brought the final and perfect revelation as viewed in John 14:16-17 ("I will ask the Father, and he will give you another Helper, to be with you forever, even the Spirit of Truth, whom the world cannot receive, because it neither sees him nor knows him".) Muhammad preached that he was the one Jesus was talking about, the Helper whom he would send; thus, in line with the prophecy, Muhammad was the Holy Spirit — not divine in nature, but holy by calling and life.

Armed with knowledge of the Qur'an, a rudimentary but effective knowledge of the Bible, and a gift for rhetoric, I made my first forays into public dialogue with Christians. For *muhadhara* events in East Africa, Muslims send around an announcement and invite Christians to discuss with them in public on a prepared topic, like "Jesus and Muhammad: who is greater?" The event opens with an imam speaking on the topic, and then response from Christians is welcomed. Initially, I was part of the group involved in dialogue after the preaching.

I quickly found myself filled with a passion for these debates. It was so easy to state our pillar that there is one God and Muhammad is his prophet, and when Christians began to elevate Jesus, we claimed they were being polytheistic. Christians generally failed to be able to discuss the Trinity with any degree of confidence, and I delighted in mocking them. They knew that the divinity of Jesus was important, while also knowing it was crucial not to publicly defend polytheism — like the African traditional religions. Ironically, almost all of the Muslims in the Gisenyi area were also practitioners of traditional African religion with its many gods.

But what really mattered in these debates was not truth or proof, or even faithfulness to one's profession, but the ability to shame the opponent. In this I soon became a master. The same self-confidence and ability to project power that had given me an intimidating presence in school also served in defeating Christians in *muhadhara*. And I loved it. I loved the feeling of making a Christian look silly or confused or afraid.

My knowledge of the Qur'an and abilities in the *muhadhara* events was noticed by the Islamic community of Gisenyi and by the students of the school. In what I thought would be a major turning point in my life, I was selected as the head of the Muslim students and put forward as an *imam* for the mosque of the school and its surrounding area. An *imam* is a leader of the prayers in a mosque and a teacher of Islam for the community. For me, this meant I would be putting my memorization of the Qur'an to daily use, guiding the mosque in prayers. Except for one short moment in the prayers, Muslims are reciting passages of the Qur'an in Arabic, not speaking to God from their hearts or heads as Christians tend to think of prayer. One of the *imam's* roles is to prompt and guide these recitations. Beyond this, my position was as an organizer of *muhadhara* debates and a teacher of the Muslim students.

Even as I was growing in my passion for Islam and in my standing in the Muslim community, I was still personally bound to drug use. I was convinced that in order to have a clear head and effective communication, I needed a smoke of marijuana every day. I was no longer selling it or using it as a form of defiance, but the thought that I could live without it was as far from the realm of possibility as the idea that I would one day be a Christian. What mattered was public perception, keeping up the appearance of honor. I looked and lived the part of an imam — no more dreads and Rasta cap, but a long robe and *kufi* cap. I believed fully that I had become who I was supposed to be, Swidiq Kanana, a builder of the House of Islam.

Chapter Eleven

"HE WHO DIGS A PIT..."

THROUGH THE YEARS of supporting my mother and siblings, I had filled the role of provider and protector for our fatherless family. That role became all the more intensified through devotion to Islam and the elevation of my status in the Muslim community. As I have explained, males in Islam possess all the roles of power and control in both family and community. It is not surprising, then, that many Muslim women take advantage of alternate forms of power — potions, charms, and sorcery — to gain some measure of invisible control in their households. In my own family, though, my sisters were asserting themselves in another direction: they were forming relationships with Christians.

Since her primary school, my younger sister Lydia had become friends with a Christian girl whose family had compassion on her due to the suffering of our family. She had been a toddler when we fled during the genocide, and when I went to the streets, she would come see me while other children her age were going to kindergarten. When I started selling drugs and brought some money home to the family, we finally sent her to school. She was in P4 when she made a new best friend, whose family always welcomed her to spend time with them. They shared their love and encouraged her at a time when there was no encouragement to be found anywhere else. She was quickly drawn to the Jesus they knew.

When she began to follow Jesus, her whole sense of self shifted. She stopped using her Muslim name and chose instead to be called Florence, the name of her friend's mother, who cared for her with tenderness. Not long after she had been baptized, I returned to Gisenyi from ETO Kicukiro in Kigali. When I soon learned of her new allegiance, I persecuted her terribly. I tried to force her to renounce Jesus — threatening to throw her out of the house and leave her begging in the streets — and if I saw her appearing to pray, I would throw her to the ground and hit or kick her. But with a dauntless boldness in the face of pain, she declared that she was willing to die for Jesus. I assured myself this was just a phase, that Lydia would come to her senses when she needed school fees. She wasn't old enough to be a public embarrassment just yet.

More serious in my mind, though, was that my oldest sister had begun spending time with a Christian young man. As the head of my household, I would not allow the shame of a sister marrying a Christian to come on my house. Initially, I welcomed him to our house and tried subtlety. Muslims are not generally known for calm, conversational persuasion in our *da'wah*, but for her sake and the possibility of his conversion, I made the effort. When I was not able to persuade him to become a Muslim, I threatened his life if he continued seeing her. I made clear to her that she would only ever marry a Muslim.

She was showing too much strength of will, so it was time to act. Both of my sisters were old enough to marry according to Rwandan law. Through connections in the Muslim community, I located a sheikh looking for a wife, and I forced her to marry him. I found him to be strict and consistent in his application of the Qur'an. And if he treated her like a slave, it was within his rights. I was fairly sure that whatever ill she experienced, it was due to her showing too much will. For the younger sister I did the same, and within six months had both of them securely married within the House of Islam.

Towards the end of that year so full of growing intensity in my devotion to Islam, something happened that changed the course of my life forever. As the proverb says, "He who digs a pit will fall into it himself." I had been digging pits everywhere I went for a long time. And just like an unexpected fall into a pit, my halt came rather suddenly.

All the secondary schools around Gisenyi participate in Interschool Games, with competitions in various sports. I was part of our school's basketball team set to compete on Friday afternoon. After our classes ended early, I went to get ready for the game. Having taken marijuana for so many years, I was convinced that it gave more energy and focus for activities like sports. So of course as I prepared to go to the game, I smoked a quick joint.

When I reached the court and began dribbling around a bit, I felt something like a tug on my brain. The pulling became more intense, seeming like my brain was being torn in two halves. I stopped out on the court with both hands to my head, squeezing and trying to hold back whatever was happening. Then suddenly it seemed like my brain burst, and I was immediately overwhelmed by a rush of sight and sound. I stumbled around for a few moments trying to escape the roar.

When the noise stopped a moment later, I looked around me trying to get my bearings. It seemed to me that everyone around me was behaving strangely. They were acting like animals or people possessed. When a person spoke, it seemed like a growl or bellow. Movements were exaggerated, like when a child pretends to be an ape or elephant. And everyone's facial features were distorted, as in a carnival mirror. I was disgusted and horrified. There was no way I was going to stay around these mad people. I went home convinced that I had narrowly escaped from something terrible.

But even as I walked home, my thoughts were running wildly. I could not hold on to any clear perception, moving from horror to danger to fear. I went from a walk to a terrified run. When I arrived home and crouched like a hunted thing in a corner, the sensations became so overwhelming that I stopped functioning altogether. From Friday afternoon to Tuesday morning, I sat in the same place, staring silently. The family brought me food and watched as I ate absentmindedly. On Tuesday morning, my mother came in to urge me to go to school.

"Swidiq, don't you have school today?" she said, as if she didn't know. In a circuitous way she suggested, "The exams are coming soon aren't they? You always do so well. I think you want to do especially well this time, don't you?" she prodded. The mention of school seemed to connect with something.

"I left my marijuana at the school," I said excitedly. "Someone's getting it!"

"What do you mean, someone is getting it?" she asked.

"Someone's getting it! Someone is getting my marijuana!" I said, getting more excited and agitated.

"He who digs a pit..."

"It's okay, Swidiq. It's okay. Don't worry about it. It's going to be alright," she said.

Thrashing around, I began shouting, "No! Don't take it! Someone is getting my marijuana! Leave it alone!"

She left the room with me still yelling. After seeing my three days of silence, and this turn to raving, they were sure that I had lost my mind.

My mother immediately concluded that I had been bewitched, probably by my stepmother. Later in the morning she recruited some friends and guided me to a well-known witchdoctor. They took me to a place outside the town known to be a sacred place of local spirits. It was a shrine or altar to the traditional gods of the region where all the tribes had often gathered for sacrifices before Christianity and Islam had come to Kivu. She had arranged to meet a sorcerer there.

When my mother explained what had happened, the sorcerer said, "The gods of our people had chosen this Swidiq of yours to succeed you as a priest of Biheko and a witchdoctor for your clan. When he was born, he was given in answer to your sacrifices — not from this Muslim Allah. He belongs to the gods, but he has broken the bonds. He has turned from his path. This madness is their punishment. He has provoked their wrath and now he suffers. You must bring a goat and sacrifice it on his behalf. Swidiq must be present for the sacrifice."

She followed the sorcerer's counsel, and on the appointed day later that week she brought me, with a goat and all the relatives she could muster, to appease the wrath of Biheko. Although these ceremonies have much shouting and dancing, nothing brought me from my state of complete distraction. While the drums beat and the blood flowed, my mind was far away in an empty place. The sorcerer assured my mother that the effects of the sacrifice could take some time, but she took me away doubtful. The spirits seemed unwavering in their hate. As the days went by with no change, she lost faith in the sorcerer's words.

One of her friends suggested that we try a Western doctor since I had been exposed to many Western influences. She took me to Ndera Neuropsychiatric Hospital in Kigali, the only psychiatric hospital in the country. Shortly after arrival, I was given a strong sedative to quiet my mind and to keep me from being a physical danger to others. In my distraction, I would sometimes take a defensive posture, as if I were being attacked and was ready to strike back. I was still very strong from kungfu training, but the sedative took the fight out of me.

The doctors concluded that I had probably been affected by my cocaine use, and they could not give a confident prognosis for recovery. Some people recover from these psychotic episodes after a short time; some never fully recover. For several months, they kept me heavily sedated. During this period, I had occasional moments of clarity in which I knew who I was and that I was being kept in a medical facility. When I demanded to be let loose, a nurse would immediately inject me with the strong sedative, and I would slip back into nothingness.

Finally, I came to a clear moment and had an inkling of the cycle, so I kept quiet. Throughout the day I surveyed the room, considered the layout that I could see through the windowed door, and paid close attention to every movement when a nurse came to bring me food. I was beginning to plot an escape when one of the doctors happened to come for a routine check. This was the first time that an actual doctor was present when I was thinking clearly. With bored inattention, he went through a standard checklist of questions. When I was able to answer his questions with something approximating self-understanding, he paused in his rote questions and began asking more directly about what I was seeing and thinking. He realized that I was actually recovering, contacted my family, and released me into their care.

Although I was back at home and slowly recovering, I would have lapses of confusion. I would forget where I was or suffer momentary delusion. The Muslim leaders also believed I was suffering due to sorcery — someone's attempt to fight against Allah — and they sought ways to restore me to health and to my role of leadership. Their attempt to counteract my problem is revealing. As I mentioned earlier, one of the Six Articles of Islam is belief in *jinn*. While angels were created from light, *jinn* are thought to be created from smokeless fire. There are Muslim *jinn* and non-Muslim *jinn*, the latter of which form the army of Satan, the chief of the *jinn*. Thus, *jinn* are the rough equivalent of demons within Christian cosmology, with some notable differences. *Jinn* marry, have offspring, and eventually die. Whereas Christian teaching on the fallen angels is that their wills have become bound to rebellion and evil, the *jinn* of Islamic teaching retain free will and can be converted to Islam. So, as mortal, spiritual beings with free will, they can be tricked, tempted, manipulated, and controlled, even as they attempt to assert their own wills over human beings. It was against evil non-Muslim *jinn* that the Muslims saw themselves battling for control of my mind. The traditional African spirits were included in these forces of hostile *jinn*.

Since *jinn* can be controlled, a group of Muslim leaders came to our house to perform rites of exorcism. Following a customary rite, they took a Qur'an and placed it on my head, then together they began reciting the Al-Baqarah surah, the longest surah of the Qur'an. The Qur'an is understood as a totemic object, having intrinsic power to drive out non-Muslim *jinn* — something like the way Roman Catholic exorcists think about the power of consecrated bread and wine. The result of their efforts was directly counter to their intention. My delusional madness returned suddenly. As they recited, I fleetingly recall the sensation of bees swarming me with an overwhelming sound of buzzing. My family tells me that I leaped up and began beating them and driving them out of the house with kungfu. A group of policemen were called, and after a long struggle subdued me with handcuffs until I became calm.

What followed was a period of which I have no memory. I was taken to a facility for the dangerously insane and put in a secure, windowless room. Food was brought and passed to me under the door. My mother tells me that sometimes I ate part of it, but other times I just smeared it on my body or sat in it. It seems there was also no distinct latrine in the room. Although it is a lost period of my life, I am grateful to have no memories of that time, when I was reduced to the most basic level of animal existence. And like Nebuchadnezzar in his madness, I was humbled.

When 11 months had passed since my mind had snapped on the basketball court, and I was so weakened that I was not considered dangerous any longer, I was back in the care of my family. They were resigning themselves to watching me fade completely. In this hopeless situation, my mother had a Christian friend who suggested that they take a different approach to my illness.

"You've tried almost everything," she said. "Why can't you try Jesus? You know that we pray for people and they sometimes get well. Bring Swidiq to see our pastor."

Her church was an Anglican Church on the hilltop above our town, and as she said, it was widely known that when they prayed for people, especially those with emotional or psychological disturbances, they often had good results. But how could she bring me, an imam and the son of a sheikh, to a Christian church? It would be scandal, and she would even be risking harm to herself with such a brazen disregard for Muslim restrictions.

But my mother was desperate to see me well, and she was willing to take the risk. Swearing the two younger children to secrecy, she took me to the church under the cover of darkness.

"How long has he been like this?" the pastor asked.

"He's had some times of sanity since then, but he first lost his mind eleven months ago," she said. "Can you do anything? They said you have powers."

He laughed a little. "I don't have powers. No one has powers. But I know the One who does, and I can ask Him to help. Now, what have you already tried?"

"We sacrificed to Biheko. We tried the Western drugs. And the Muslims tried to exorcise *jinn* with the Qur'an," she said.

"And what happened when they tried the Qur'an?" he asked. She explained my violent response and how I seemed to lose all sense of life after that. He opened his Bible and showed her the passage after Jesus came down from the mountain of Transfiguration, and the disciples were unable to cast out a demon.

"'This kind comes out only by prayer and fasting,'" he quoted. "We'll try it, but you must know that we are only asking God to do it. It's in God's hands. We can't make him do anything. Your son has been repeatedly given to evil, and he has given himself to evil. His deliverance will come only by the mercy of Jesus."

So the pastor and a group of four others began to pray and fast. And for seven days, she brought me to the church each night. They fasted and prayed, and each night they sang songs of peace over me, laid their hands on me, and asked God to be merciful. On the seventh day, as they were praying, something happened.

I became conscious of myself. I was aware. I knew that I was trying to see but my vision was hazy. Slowly but steadily the blur was clearing, and I saw that I was in a Christian place. It was a wide room filled with low benches. In the mud-brick walls, I could see the dark shape of crosses letting in the night air. Near us at the front of this large space was a table. I could see crosses and open books. Then I began to hear sounds, at first like what you hear when you are swimming just beneath the surface of the

"He who digs a pit..."

water. And then I saw people looking at me wide-eyed and then beginning to dance and rejoice, leaping and shouting praises to God. I was too weak and overwhelmed to move or respond, but they continued to pray for me. The longer they prayed and called on the name of Jesus, the more clearly I could see and hear and know myself. I quickly realized that I had been very unwell.

"Welcome back, Swidiq," said a man in a black shirt with a bit of white at the collar. "Satan has been keeping you in a prison, but tonight Jesus has opened the door and brought you out. It seems that he has reason for you to live."

By the time they sent us home that night, I had begun to remember bits of my madness. I recalled the moment of my mind breaking. I remembered the doctor coming to release me. And I had glimpses of the paranoia and apparitions that had troubled me.

More importantly, as we walked home that night, I knew that Jesus had healed me. The pastor was clear enough on that point. My mother, too, had to acknowledge that the power of Jesus had restored my mind. The conclusion was painfully obvious and also very confusing. When every other power has been tried and has failed — pagan gods, Western medicine, and the Qur'an — only a stronger power could succeed. I was stuck with the fact: Jesus must be stronger.

Chapter Twelve

JESUS IN THE MOSQUE

WHAT FOLLOWED MY HEALING from mental illness and deliverance from demonic power was a situation faced by many Muslims around the world today. Through one way or another, a Muslim comes to see that Jesus is not merely the Prophet Jesus as taught in Islam, but somehow he is alive, divine, and desiring to interact with people. Likewise, they find that Christianity is not merely a set of beliefs and practices but an ongoing relationship with the Creator God through his own Spirit. For Muslims, among the greatest shocks is that God loves and interacts with individual people, that a man or a woman can talk to him about their feelings and concerns, and he talks back. By definition, Muslims believe that Islam is the correct explanation of God and his ways with human beings, and the gap between God and men is so great that there can be no intimate communication between them. Submission to Allah's revelation to Muhammad and obedient observance of the Five Pillars are how humans are to relate to God.[6] It is, essentially, a religion of observance and performance. In every case where a Muslim comes to a realization that there is more to Jesus than taught in Islam, that he may be divine or that he can be known personally, the realization brings about a crisis.

---

6. The Five Pillars of Islam are the declaration of faith (called the Shahada: "There is no God but Allah, and Muhammad is his prophet"); the regular performance of the five daily times of prayer; giving of alms; observance of fasting during the month of Ramadan; and a journey to Mecca once during one's lifetime.

Jesus in the Mosque

In my heart, I knew that Jesus had healed me. I recalled enough of the previous year, and my family and friends told me enough additionally, that I was absolutely certain my situation had been hopeless. Without the intervention of the Christians and the power of Jesus's name, I would have spent the rest of my life with the mentality of an animal. I had been totally broken. But how could I speak of these things to my fellow Muslims?

That I was healed no one attempted to deny. Among the family and our Muslim community, my mother kept the secret that she had taken me to the Anglican Church for prayer. We kept the truth even from my father, who concluded that healing from Allah had finally broken through a cloud of evil. Generally, the Muslims of Gisenyi posited a syncretistic explanation, that the many incantations and sacrifices had appeased the wrath of the African gods, allowing Allah's mercy to come through. So the honor and glory for the healing was given to every other deity than the one who had done it. This duplicity worked uncomfortably in me, as I felt myself in constant deceit while also betraying the mercy of Jesus.

But the impossibility of speaking the truth about my healing was overwhelming. I had been chosen by the men of my father's mosque to be the next imam and eventually sheikh. This path seemed fixed from my birth, even in my given name, and the previous two years had appeared to be the fruition, as I was among the youngest imams in all of East Africa. Even my recent bought with evil confirmed the Muslim community in their choice, as they interpreted the mental breakdown as a struggle against non-Muslim *jinn* in which I had been victorious. They believed that while I was in a state of complete distraction, I had been doing battle with evil *jinn* in the unseen world. Not only could I defeat Christians in debate and persuade many to convert to Islam, but they saw me as spiritually mighty, too. I could not bear the thought of all the shame that would come on me and on my family if I admitted we were wrong about Jesus.

As is well known to many Western Christians, the truth that I had been healed by prayers through the power of Jesus's name would have been dangerous as well. Were I to tell truly what I knew, that Jesus brings the power of God, a power greater than African spirits and greater than is available in Islam, I would run the risk of being silenced — physically and forever. While Muslims will tolerate and even embrace the practices of paganism and the propitiation of lesser spirits, they will not abide even the hint of Jesus's divinity within their community. In particular, if someone in prominence, such as an imam, reveals any allegiance to Jesus, he will be put to death as the worst kind of poison to the Muslim community. From their perspective, it is enacting their commitment to preserving the community from dangerous teaching and apostasy. To rid the mosque of such poison is for the good of all. So with the fear of man filling my heart, I held steady in Islam, all the while knowing that Jesus can heal.

I had not yet encountered God in any personal way. It would be better to say that I had been the subject and beneficiary of healing rather than a participant in it. Jesus had heard the prayers of his people and had acted. But in these days of doubt and confusion for me, I began to pray on my own behalf.

As I have explained about *salaat*, the times of daily prayer, the ritual is almost entirely recitation. The prayers are general, meant to shape an attitude and life of submission, resulting in peace and comfort. Christians often speak of liturgy in this way, and the *salaat* liturgy of prayer definitely shapes the lives, habits, and daily rhythms of Muslims. But in contrast to the typical Christian notion of prayer, understanding is not necessary for piety — the act of participation itself is pious. These prayers are not a personal conversation with the infinite God. Yet, in *salaat* there is a space for free prayer, for bringing personal petitions before Allah, although with no thought that he would speak back in that time or any other time. In these moments, I began to speak to Jesus about my situation.

These prayers began to take shape as I would drift mentally into the agony of my dilemma. I first started asking Allah why he gave Jesus power to heal me but not to save me from Muslims who would not believe it. I wondered to Allah if Muslims could be convinced that Jesus is more than a prophet. But as I began speaking to Allah in this way, prayers started leaping to my mind, bursting out from deep inside. More importantly, I was speaking to someone else. I found myself imploring Jesus to make his power known. I wanted him to have the glory he deserved. And more and more I mourned for my situation of preserving a lie that robbed Jesus of his honor, while keeping me in a position of respect.

The thing that I feared eventually came upon me. I was called to be the debating imam against a group of Christians at an upcoming *muhadhara* event. My role, as always, would be to argue against the claims of Jesus and instead urge the honor of Muhammad and the power of the Qur'an. I could not do it. I could not speak against Jesus anymore. While I had very little idea what was true of him, I knew that I could not say Muhammad is greater or that the Qur'an is more powerful than the name of Jesus. It wasn't true.

To avoid the impossible moment, the morning of the *muhadhara* I resorted to desperate and ridiculous measures. I wrapped my body in paper to trap my body heat. With my wrappings hidden under clothes and a blanket, I heated up as if I had a high fever. When my father came to walk with me to the event, he found me burning up in bed. Not wanting to aggravate my condition, he went along without me to express my regrets that I was too sick to speak.

Not long after escaping the debate, I was back in the Islamic school to finish up my long-delayed secondary schooling. I was still guiding Muslim students, teaching them the Qur'an and the traditions of Muhammad. But I felt like a fraud. All the while I kept feeling a terrible dissonance. I was playing a role and pretending. I was declaring and teaching the way of Islam, but I wasn't sure what was true, except the growing reality that Jesus is real.

For me, this situation continued for seven months from the time of my healing until it came to a startling conclusion. For many other Muslims around the world, this terrible position of unstable and confusing identity persists for years. Some have read parts of the New Testament given to them by Christians and have been startled to find themselves confessing Jesus. Others have come in contact with Christians and have had their assumptions undermined, gradually coming to see Christianity differently and encountering Jesus through the words and testimony of Christians. Still others have had dreams or waking visions of a divine being, who reveals himself to be the risen Jesus Christ. Whatever the cause for acknowledging the ultimate rule of Jesus, they find themselves as believers in Jesus inside the mosque. This conjunction is a painful state.

Particularly for women, there may be no place where they can escape. While a man may be able to find a way to extricate himself and his family from the community, Muslim women who find Jesus are held by love and duty to their children and husband. Sometimes the laws of their land make no provision for a change in faith; some laws even obligate their husbands to kill them. Frequently, their husbands discover their new faith, yet they are still compelled to follow the Pillars of Islam and are threatened with death if they make their belief public.

For these women and for many men, the fear of death, the loss of family, or even just not knowing how to join with Christians can keep them in a state of anxious, dual identity for years. In this position, away from the household of Christ and the protection of that gathered flock, they are easily subject to the condemnations of the evil one. Satan brings accusation and speaks with condemnation, trying to convince the new believer that Jesus will reject them and that the Christian community will not want anything to do with them. The threat is utter isolation. These believers inside the mosque need our prayers. They need to know that Jesus will embrace them. And we need to pray that Christians around them will welcome them without fear and provide the spiritual protection they need, as well as provide for the physical needs that will arise when they make their confession of Christ.

Chapter Thirteen

THE UNDISCOVERED COUNTRY

SINCE MY MENTAL RESTORATION and insight into the power of Jesus, I had passed seven months in the turmoil of wanting to know Jesus from inside the mosque. Christians from the Anglican Church would stop me on the road or visit me secretly to encourage me to leave Islam and come into the Church of Jesus Christ. They little understood what this move would mean for me, and they could not understand that I lacked the power in my own will to break the bonds that held me.

As I was back in school finishing up my secondary school work, I was sitting in class one day when something in my gut began to go wrong. Without warning, I felt a tearing inside my abdomen. It seemed as if my organs were being pulled apart. Taking breath felt like a knife cutting as my expanding lungs pushed on the organs. I tried to stop breathing. Every little intake of breath felt like razors. I fell on the ground foaming at the mouth. The teacher rushed to get help as my classmates gathered around me.

I was taken to the hospital in Gisenyi for x-rays, hunched over to keep from taking a deep breath. When the time for x-rays came, I cried with the pain as I had to stretch out on my back. To everyone's dismay, the x-rays showed no abnormality. Again, man's wisdom was failing. The doctors quickly transferred me to Ruhengeri Hospital, the main district hospital of Musanze district. There was a white doctor there, whom people had nicknamed Buzima, meaning "Life," because he had brought back hope for life to so many people of the region. He had been in Rwanda for decades and had come to understand that there were things that Western medicine would never be able to cure.

My father went with me to see this Buzima in Ruhengeri. He examined me, applied acupuncture, gave me some medication for pain, and conducted several scans. After he looked at all the information he had collected, he came to talk with my father while I lay crumpled on the bed.

"You can see that things are very bad," he said. "But there is nothing particular that I can point to. The scans of his abdomen show no abnormal growths, no tearing. There's no inflammation, no infection. No obvious medical cause. Could it be…" and he paused.

"Could it be what?" my father said.

"It may be one of the things of Africa. Has there been a curse? Is there an enemy?"

"It may be," my father answered. He was thinking of my step-mother.

"Well, there is nothing I can do. But if it is a matter of Africa, then I suggest you try the treatments of Africa. Something will have to change. His short intakes of breath, drawn in like he's doing…. His lungs will debilitate within two weeks. That's it. He has to start breathing again."

There was a note of finality about his assessment. As I lay there, overhearing the conversation, I knew I was going to die. I had heard of bewitching like this before. Always it was described like I was feeling, like cutting, like razors or knives. I was certain I had been either poisoned or cursed. Either way, the result would be the same. I was going to die.

My father took me home. At this point in his life, he had concluded one thing about traditional African religion and medicine: it could bring evil but not good. Instead, he sought an appointment at the best hospital in Rwanda, King Faisal Hospital in Kigali. With a referral from the doctor in Musanze, he obtained an emergency appointment with an Australian doctor at King Faisal.

The doctor ran a battery of tests and performed several scans with the most advanced technologies available in East Africa. One set of scans revealed blood clotting throughout my capillaries, which was now beginning in the larger vessels as well. The clotting was so complete that it was closing down the veins entirely. The doctor concluded that I had some type of highly aggressive blood cancer. He took my father aside to speak privately.

"I wish I had better news," he said matter-of-factly. "It's possible that he might respond to some powerful blood thinner to stop the advance of the clotting, but even that probably wouldn't do very much. The reality is, he's too weak for the blood thinner. It would kill him before the clotting will."

"What can you do? Is this it?" my father asked weakly.

"I think it's time to be palliative," he said.

"I'm sorry, what is palliative?"

"It means I can give him a powerful pain reliever to make his passing easier on him."

"I see," my father said. "I will take him home."

When my father stepped back to where I lay, curled in a fetal position on the bed of the examining room, I saw the news on his face. I knew my death was near. He stood silently beside me for a moment, his face testing out various expressions as he searched for what to say. Finally, he settled on something.

"You know what the old men say, 'You can outrun what's chasing you, but you can't outrun what's inside you'? . . . The old are always right," he said, trying to end with a smile. "Let us go home."

The long journey home was full of swirling thoughts, punctuated by physical pain. As we sped along the road, the fields of rice in the valleys around Kigali gave way to valleys lush with the brilliant green of tea plantations. Women in bright head-scarves waded through the waving green seas, plucking the pekoes and tossing them in baskets on their backs. Ribbons of dusty red wound their way up slope after slope, cutting through terraces of deep green potato plants, beans, and peas. It was the short rainy season, and the whole land was at the peak of life and vibrance. I felt what many have felt before, the indifference of the land for one passing through it and the utter disregard of the world for the suffering of its own.

Yes, Rwanda is truly a beautiful land, the land of a thousand hills. And as I passed from Kigali to Gisenyi, for what I believed was the last time, bitter tears wet my face that it cared nothing for me.

At home, my entire body was in agonizing pain. Every touch, every nerve seemed to sear like fire playing over my skin. Each breath continued to be a torture. I feared falling into sleep because breathing would deepen, and I would jolt alert again with unendurable stabs to the chest and gut. I wanted to die. I wanted the pain to end.

My father brought the medicine — the palliative care the doctor spoke of — and I managed to get it down. Within about fifteen minutes, a strange sensation began at my spine and crept out to my extremities. I felt heavy. Then I tried to lift my hand and found that I couldn't. I tried to move my leg, but it did not respond. Even my fingers refused to wiggle. Terror crept over me. I was paralyzed. Completely. But what made the terror worse was that the pain remained.

For several days I persisted in this desperate state of fear, pain, and exhaustion. I couldn't speak, and because my neck was paralyzed, I could only stare in one direction. My family kept moving nutrients into me through a tube in my nose. I was not able to tell them to stop and just let me die. I tried to speak with my eyes, but it only seemed to trouble them with pained compassion.

On the evening of February 27, about 8pm, I became terribly alert. A horrible sensation like nothing I had known was washing over me. I seemed to be wrapped in fire, billowing all around me and burning without consuming. Even to this day, the memory is inextricably connected to thoughts and images of hell, a fire that is never quenched. I felt terribly thirsty, but there was no way to beg for a drink. I tried to move, tried to communicate in some way, any way. But I was totally paralyzed. To suffer so horribly without any way to call for help added to the desperate fear. I was sweating so profusely that I had drenched all my clothes, and when my mother passed through the room, she noticed the soaking clothes and called for others to come.

As people came rushing into the room, I felt as if my heart were seized and jerked. There was a steady and irresistible tugging, until my heart seemed to be pulled up, out through my mouth. It was a strange sensation but not a painful one, spiritual rather than physical. Almost at the same time, something like a strong wind was sweeping me, drawing me away from my body. And then I went. I was gone from my body. Dying itself was not nearly so bad as the process leading up to it. It was very . . . seamless.

Immediately, I seemed to fall down into an enclosed room. It was a room with no doors, but large windows lined one wall. As I looked, one of the windows opened by itself. From outside, from wherever or whatever was outside, four horrific figures stepped one at a time onto the sill and jumped down into the room. They were in the shape of men, each one wearing a long, black robe covered and dripping with blood. The bloody robes draped so low that they revealed only vilely long and hooked toenails. Each figure had black, vacant eyes and sharp fangs like a vampire, with blood dripping from its mouth. In gnarled hands with jagged talons for fingernails, each one carried an implement. One had a small hand-scythe, one held a sword, one carried a double-edged axe, and the last swung an old bucket. They were sickening and terrifying to behold.

As they came, they were dancing and singing inhuman words. They growled to each other with sounds like animals, sounds that came from inside them but that seemed far from human communication or the gift of speech. The demon carrying the bucket and the one with the scythe set down their tools and attacked me, forcing me to the ground. The one with the bucket held my arms stretched out above my head, while the other spirit grasped my legs. The other two continued with their dance, now leaping and dancing on top of me. They seemed to mock me, as in all of this I was defenseless. I was entirely in their power and subject to their destructive aims.

The two dancing spirits paused their activity, and the spirit with the axe stood over me, with one foot on my stomach. He settled the axe into his hands and rested the blade on my chest, just as you choose your place on a log before splitting it. He lifted the axe high over his head.

As I winced, the evil spirits suddenly stopped, and all looked towards the windows. Someone else had entered. Though I could not immediately see him come, I felt him enter just as they did. As I turned my head, I saw sandaled feet and a white robe. In the presence of this man, I completely forgot about the others, who fell back dismayed and then seemed to evaporate. I was captivated by him, totally uninterested in anything else but the sight of this person.

The one now standing in the room, wearing a long white robe, looked just like the Jesus of *The Passion of the Christ*, the film by Mel Gibson. I had once gotten a deal for three American films dubbed in Kinyarwanda, and the first one in the lineup had been *The Passion*. Although I was a Muslim and had no interest in seeing the Jesus story, I had gone ahead to get my full money's worth. And now he stood there, looking at me. His face was serious and intent on me — the kind of expression that holds absolute authority — but the flicker of a smile or perhaps delight played across all his features. He stood a moment just looking at me. Whether it was just an instant or a long time, I don't really know. I had not the least inclination to say anything or to move; it was perfect contentment to simply look at him.

I also don't think it was in my power to do anything but look at him. At some point, he lifted his hands slightly, with palms up, revealing holes in each hand. Then he raised his right hand and gestured towards me.

With lifted hand at last he spoke, clear and firm. "I died for man. And you are among those I died for. Do not deny it again. You must tell others. Reveal it." I am telling you in English, but Jesus spoke Kinyarwanda. Then he disappeared.

When he was gone, I glanced quickly around me. The other spirits were nowhere to be found, and though I looked about the room, there was no trace of them or their implements of horror. The presence of Jesus had cleansed every mark of their visit.

And then, like the force that had pulled me from my body, I felt a sweeping pressure from behind. I was surging powerfully and suddenly upward, like emerging from the depths of the water when you have dived deep. I was rushing upward toward light, and suddenly I stopped. I had entered my body again. I coughed and opened my eyes. I sat up, pulled a sheet off, and stood up.

Chapter Fourteen

A NEW LEASE

TOSSING THE SHEET ASIDE, I stood for a moment next to a table on which I had been lying, not recalling anything of the experience that had just passed. People were wildly running in all directions, glancing back over their shoulders with frightened expressions and yelling. My thinking was fuzzy, and I could not understand what was happening. Dazed, I followed them outside, wondering to myself, "Why are they running?" Slipping back to an old pattern of thought, I posited that perhaps my father was using them to play a trick on me, or maybe there was witchcraft going on.

As I looked around outside, I saw people with shovels standing next to a large hole and also staring at me with shocked expressions. I thought perhaps they were digging a pit for a toilet, maybe for a wedding celebration. Uninterested and still not grasping the meaning of what was going on, I turned passively back towards the house.

There on a table that I must have walked past, I saw all the items for the ritual cleaning of a dead body. In East Africa, Muslims perform several rituals on the body of a deceased person. Before the body is buried — always on the day immediately following the death — they wash the body thoroughly in accordance with Islamic custom everywhere. While washing, certain phrases are said for each part of the body. After the outside of the body is washed three times, the inside of the body must be cleansed as well. They bring boiling water and pour it down the throat, filling the body cavity completely. Then they press on the abdomen so that the water courses through the digestive tract and washes out the uncleanness. When I saw the table, with the steaming hot water ready for the final step of interior cleansing, it finally occurred to me, "Someone has died."

It was just at that point that I realized I was almost naked, wearing only a small loin cloth, the customary covering for the ritual washing. Like an electric shock, all the pieces fell suddenly into place. "Someone died. I'm naked. They're running. I must have been dead."

Feeling suddenly shy and awkward, I turned to go into the house, but the doorway was full of astonished people watching my every movement. There in the middle of the crowd was a face I recognized. It was Jesus Christ. He looked at me intently, with the same fixed expression of authority with the unaccountable hint of mirth playing across his features. Again he raised his hand and pointed to me, now giving me a knowing smile. All other sound ceased to my ears as I heard him say, "Do you remember?" Then he was gone.

The whole experience came rushing back as I vividly recalled the moments I had passed in that other place beyond death. I began shouting, "Jesus is here! Jesus is here! He is among us!" And when the people seemed not to understand, I kept on, "He brought me back! It was Jesus who got me and brought me back!"

That was too much for this crowd of terrified Muslims. They began running hysterically in all directions.

I was shouting after them, "Don't go! Jesus is here! He can save you. He has saved me. Don't you see, I'm alive!" As I was shouting, I noticed Benimana Jean-Claude, the Anglican pastor who had prayed for my mental healing. In small places like where we lived, everyone hears when someone has died, and Jean-Claude had come to honor me and show his care for the family. Quickly understanding what was happening, he joined me in declaring the power and love of Jesus, adding that forgiveness was available for all.

My friend Abdullah, who was the *muezzin* — the one who calls the people to the times of prayer — was not looking carefully as he ran. He fell right into the grave that had been dug for me. Stuck in the earth, he could hear my voice calling out that Jesus saves from evil and death. There he was, in the grave of a man who had been paralyzed and had died but was now alive and well, and the truth conquered him.

As I continued to call out that Jesus is the one who can defeat death, and that he has power over every evil and has died for people, a number of my Muslim family and friends began to come out from behind buildings where they had hidden themselves. Abdullah managed to pull himself out of the grave. He was the first to move towards us. He came to Pastor Jean-Claude and knelt at his feet, asking for prayer to become a Christian.

Seeing Abdullah's kneeling and submitting to the authority of Jesus, others began to come close as the pastor guided them to receive mercy. My own mother was among the thirty-one Muslims kneeling with Jean-Claude.

As the circle was gathering, I heard the drums begin to roll out the call to worship at the Anglican Church on the hill, Pastor Jean-Claude's church. This custom dates back to the East African Revival of the 1930s, as the gospel made its way into the valleys and villages of Rwanda, Uganda, and Burundi.[7] The drums would announce to all those in earshot that the Bible would be read and explained, and people came to hear the Word of life. To this day, all across Rwanda, the drums of the Anglican Church begin about 9:15am on Sunday morning, and they keep rolling as people make their long walks to the local church, singing as they come.

When I heard those drums, my heart leapt, "You belong there!" Heedless that I was dressed in only a burial loin cloth, I went running across the valley and up the hill.

When at last I rounded the hilltop, most of the congregation had already filled the church building. A teenage girl who had been drumming the call to worship looked up and recognized me. Shrieking, she darted into the church. I took a deep breath and followed her in.

I stood at the back, not knowing what I should do now. As the girl ran ahead of me down the center aisle, a cascade of turning heads and gasps followed her heels. They had already announced that the son of the sheikh had died, so when they saw me coming into their worship, they were not sure what to think. Soon the whole congregation was standing and gawking at where I stood by the doorway, uncertain. Some thought I was a ghost while others were certain I was a demon. A group huddled to discuss how to deal with me. Then they broke huddle and came towards

---

7. For accounts of the East African Revival, see *The East African Revival: History and Legacies* (Routledge, 2012), edited by Kevin Ward and Emma Wild Wood.

me together.

"In the name of Jesus, we cast you out," they said. "If you are the spirit of Swidiq, we send you now to your place of rest. If you are Satan's messenger, we cast you to the pit!"

In the mercies of God, Pastor Jean-Claude arrived at just that moment. He had seen me running towards the church and had followed as quickly as he could.

"No, no! Don't be afraid! This is no spirit. This is really Swidiq!" As he spoke and began to explain, he raised his hands and continued with a swaying dance of praise, showing clearly that all he said was to the glory of God. "Do you remember when we were praying for the healing of his mind? I had a dream — I told you of it. I saw him preaching to a crowd of many races. And the Lord said, 'He will preach where you cannot reach.' Remember?"

The people were still too stunned to speak, so he continued.

"When I heard of his death last night, I wondered what it might mean. I was sure the dream was from the Lord. So I wondered, 'Maybe somehow his death will preach.' And it was so!" He leaped in the air with visible punctuation. "It was so! The Lord Jesus came personally and brought him back — totally well — and he sent him back preaching. Today he has preached to the Muslims even without knowing the Bible!"

The reality of what had happened was dawning on the people, and a young man ran to the drums, grabbed the sticks, and began pounding out a rhythm for a dance of praise. The music seemed to settle the truth into place. Jean-Claude took up the dance, and the whole congregation joined him dancing and singing, leading me down to the front of the church. When the dance concluded, the pastor set me in a front chair next to him, while another man began to preach.

The sermon was from John 5:1-10, about the man by the pool of Bethesda who had been sick for 38 years. The lay preacher described how nothing had helped him — friends, family, knowledge, religion — nothing could heal him. "That's me," I thought. "He is talking about me." I was on the edge of my seat as he then recounted how Jesus came to the man by the pool and asked him if he wanted to be made well. In my mind I answered for him, "Yes! Yes! I want to be well."

By way of illustration, the preacher brought out a small floor mat. Concluding his message, he gestured to the mat at his feet. "There is a place here, like the pool, where you can be healed. Just like at the pool of Bethesda, the Lord Jesus offers healing to those who want to be well. Come forward and receive prayer. This will be the first step of your healing."

In Islamic thought, when the tradition has established a teaching, it is fixed. All hermeneutics, preaching, and explication are exactly literal according to the tradition. So if the preacher said the mat was the same as the pool, then I concluded that in Christianity the mat at the front of the church must be the place of healing in Christian worship. In the passage, the first person into the pool of Bethesda would be healed; it must be the same here. So I was ready, watching, making sure I would be the first in. I even planned some kungfu moves to make sure nobody would beat me there. As soon as he said, "Come," I dove to the mat! First one in!

Others came, and ministers gathered around to guide us in prayer. When they prayed for me, an overwhelming torrent of tears burst from deep inside and poured from my eyes. There were too many sobs to speak through. Pastor Jean-Claude and another minister guided me to a side room to talk more and pray more. They guided me to understand that Jesus had moved towards me and had offered me new life. Because of his own death on the cross, he took death and judgment for me, and clearly he loved me and was offering salvation. My work was trust him. I needed to accept the forgiveness he offered.

Through the sobs, I said, "Yes, yes, I want forgiveness! Forgive me, Jesus!" I felt a tremendous lightness filling me inside. It was like joyous laughing in my soul that bubbled out. So as the tears subsided, I still struggled to speak through the laughter and joy.

We returned to the worship as others were testifying to what the Lord had done in them. When I had the opportunity, I stood in front of the congregation — still in the loin cloth! — and made confession of my faith. I told briefly about how Jesus had saved me through their prayers, and how I had been afraid to confess him. And I told how in my death Jesus had come and commanded me not to deny him any longer. I confessed that Jesus is Lord and that he had died for me, and I received his love and forgiveness. I was so full of joy that I kept having to suppress laughter as I spoke.

When I finished, a woman came and wrapped me around the waist with a *kitenge*, the same sort of long cloth I had first used to smuggle drugs. There was something of God in her action. I was being re-clothed. The old Swidiq had died, someone new had been reborn. This woman and her *kitenge* were like a swaddling.

With Jean-Claude holding my hand, I walked home after the worship knowing that everything had just changed. I was beginning a new life as a saved one. I had been dead for twelve hours, from 9pm on Saturday to 9am on Sunday. It seems that time in the realms of spirit do not work the same as terrestrial time. Some days later I realized that my return to life that Sunday, my spiritual rebirth, was also on my birthday, February 28.

Whatever happened in the spiritual also had affected the physical. I was completely well. Just as the presence of Jesus had completely broken the power of the evil spirits, his presence had completely broken the power of what had caused my death. There was no pain, no problem breathing, no blood cancer, and no desire for drugs. It was as if the Lord Jesus had remodeled and renovated my house, cleaning out the dark spaces and repairing what had been destroyed. He made it a place for himself, a place for his Spirit to dwell. "Behold, he is coming, and he makes all things new!"

Chapter Fifteen

IMMIGRANT EDUCATION

ANYONE WHO HAS MOVED from their own country to a new land knows the process of having to learn a new culture. The laws are new and strange, the customs do not always make sense, and the social norms can be disorienting. Often immigrants will draw analogies from their homeland to try to understand the new country, frequently making mistakes in the process. For example, when Western visitors to East Africa leave the large cities, they immediately notice they are the object of stares. When males from Northern or Western European descent experience these stares, they feel threatened because those cultures communicate challenges through stares. In East Africa, though, a stare is neutral and normal. In Rwanda especially, whenever a person encounters a stranger, including other Rwandans, he or she will stare at the newcomer, pondering where they might be from, whether they might have some type of family connection, why they might be visiting, etc. Likewise, it is not considered rude to watch another person's activity. For visitors, it takes some getting used to. Immigrants from any country moving to a new land have to pass through this kind of cultural adjustment; it's a necessary part of adopting a new culture.

While I went home to the same house the night of my rebirth, I went home as an immigrant in a strange new land. Little did I know that the Lord had called me to become like Abraham, walking in faith as a citizen of heaven. As a citizen in the kingdom of Jesus, I had to learn about my new king and his kingdom. I had to learn how his people live and how they relate to the nation of their sojourning. Like any immigrant, it was not always a smooth process.

In the first few days after I had been reborn, I soaked in a profound and strange joy and peace. Flowing over me and through me, the sensations seemed almost tangible. It was all so good that I wanted everyone I knew to experience this same joy and deep delight. I had always been a zealous person, bringing my will fully to bear on whatever I committed to. I knew that if I had been zealous for Islam, which brought only fleeting moments of comfort amidst endless striving, how much more ought I to be zealous to proclaim Jesus, who brought ever-deepening joy and peace!

I went to convert my oldest friend, Faraji. He had, of course, been there through the night of my death and through the funeral preparations. He had helped to dig my grave. With all the rest, he had been terrified and astonished at my reawakening, and he had run from the declarations about Jesus. I knew he would not want to hear about Jesus, so I prepared myself for evangelism in the way that I had always known: persuasion by any means. When Faraji opened his door, I stepped inside. Then I pulled out a knife!

Brandishing the knife, I said forcefully but smilingly, "Faraji, you cannot run from Jesus anymore. I want you to feel the joy I feel! You can't imagine what it's like! Complete peace. Hope for the future. It seems like nothing could take this joy away. Nothing. Everything will be good. You need this! You must convert."

"Swidiq, no. I'm a Muslim. There is no God but Allah, and Muhammad is his prophet," Faraji said.

I was not willing for my dearest friend to keep away from Jesus, so I came close to him, shoving the knife near his body. I said, "You must say the truth. You must confess Jesus is your savior. Now, bow!"

In terror for his life, Faraji knelt down and bowed his head to the ground. I imitated the Christians who had prayed for me and knelt beside him with one hand gently on his head. The other hand held the knife so he could see it.

I commanded, "Now say, 'Jesus, you are the Lord and you are my savior.'"
Faraji complied, "Jesus, you are the Lord and you are my savior."
Then I prayed that Faraji would feel the great peace that I felt and that

he would be filled with the great joy that had filled me.

Obviously, this was not the way to go about proclaiming Jesus and inviting loved ones into the Kingdom. And the church was quick to correct me and help me see the errors in compulsory conversion. Picturing Jesus holding a knife to the woman at the well or the rich young ruler, I had to admit the absurdity. But amazingly, strangely, mercifully, and in spite of my error, Faraji really was converted and really did feel the peace and joy of the Lord Jesus! When he was baptized, he took the Christian name Paul. Not only has he kept the faith, he is now an evangelist in the Kivu region of Rwanda.

About two weeks after my visit to Faraji, I was at home in the same room where I had died, lying down to sleep. I heard a clear, resounding knock at the door. I hopped up and opened the door, but there was nobody there. Figuring that my mother or brother had come but had decided to let me sleep, I lay down again. My eyes were just becoming drowsy when something caused them to fly wide open. Straight above me on the ceiling, I saw clearly written, as if in light, the words in our language of Kinyarwanda, "Look! I stand at the door and knock." I leaped up and ran to the door, flinging it wide open. But there was no one there, and it did not seem that anyone was stirring in the house. When I looked back to the ceiling, the words were gone.

In the morning, I told my mother about what had happened, but she had not heard anything or seen anything strange. She suggested I go see the Anglican pastor and ask him what it could mean. Later in the morning, I went and found him at his home next to the church. He flipped through his Bible and came to somewhere near the back. He pointed to the page and asked me to read verse 20 in the third chapter. I saw that it was a book called Revelation. And there it was, the same words I had seen on my ceiling, "Look! I stand at the door and knock." I read the rest of the words of the verse, "If any one hears my voice and opens the door, I will come in and eat with him, and he with me" (Rev. 3:20).

"What does it mean?" I asked. "What is he saying? I went to the door, but there was nobody there. And it was my sleeping room."

"When God speaks, he is usually speaking about the most important things, but he uses ideas we can relate to. So when he says he will come eat with you, he is talking about the kind of relationship that is formed while we eat together. You know, the love we feel. The friendship of eating. Like when you invite a friend for a meal. You share, he shares. You trust each other."

"I see, so what do you think he wants me to do? God doesn't eat food," I said.

"I think he wants a special time with you. He wants you to know him. Next time he visits, just say, 'I hear you, my Master,'" Jean-Claude said.

I understood his point. Yielding to God made perfect sense to a former Muslim. What was hard to grasp and fully accept was that Jesus, this divine person, would want to speak to me and have friendship. From a Muslim perspective, it was a ridiculous notion — the immortal, invisible, almighty one mixing with filthy mortals. But when I listened again to the voice of Jesus in my memory, and I came to the place of peace and recalled what I knew truly about him, I could see the truth of it. Somehow, for reasons known only to himself, this all-powerful being wanted to know and be known by humans. He had taken the initiative to come find me under the power of death and in the bonds of evil, and he had called me among the redeemed.

That night, I took my plate of food into the bedroom. Our small house did not have a dining room or kitchen table like an American or British house. Rwandan kitchens are traditionally outside the main house in an anterior structure, so we sit with our bowl or plate pretty much anywhere in the house. As I sat on the bed ready to eat, I felt the atmosphere of the room shift somehow. I looked up to see Jesus enter the room, passing through the closed door.

At the first instant, I was afraid, wondering, "Have I done wrong?" In Islamic belief, jinn will attack you if you wrong them in some way or take something they want. For a brief instant, the thought raced through my mind, "Maybe Jesus is going to attack me?" I was seated on the bed, so in my fear I thought to escape. I backed away along the edge of the bed. But he walked steadily forward. I kept backing away until I ran into the wall. There was nowhere else for me to run.

As he came forward, though, his peace came with him. Amid that holiness, it may sound odd, but Jesus was holding a toothbrush. I was frozen as he came closer, and with a swift motion he put the toothbrush in my mouth and promptly disappeared. Immediately, I started speaking loudly and rapidly with words I did not understand.

My mother heard me and came to check on me. Finding me babbling unintelligibly, she thought I had lost my mind again. I was lost in an exhilaration of speech and did not even notice her coming or that she pulled me close to her. When the flow of words finally subsided, I found myself held in her arms.

"You were speaking strangely," she said. "I know what Arabic sounds like, and what English and French sound like, but I've never heard anything like what you were speaking. How are you feeling? Is your mind okay? Do you know me?"

I assured her that I was perfectly conscious and told her about the vision, and we decided it was best to seek the pastor again and see what this could mean. The thought crossed my mind that when Muhammad received his first visions, he worried that he had been possessed by evil jinn. The sound of bells had rung in his ears, while he foamed at the mouth and bellowed like a camel. It was his wife Kadijah who assured him the revelations were from Allah. Now that I knew she was wrong and his revelations were false, I wondered about my own vision and this strange speaking. I clung to the simple things I knew: it was the same Jesus I had seen in death, and it was the same joy and peace. In Muhammad's visions, he had only fear, no joy.

Sitting in Pastor Jean-Claude's front room, we told him about the experience. My mother expressed her concern that I had slipped back into madness momentarily. Before giving his thoughts, Pastor Jean-Claude said we ought to pray. He began to pray, asking the Lord for wisdom, and then he started praying in another language. Before I knew what was happening, I found myself speaking right along with him. Again, there was a delight and peace in the prayer, even though I had no notion what I was saying. The words continued to flow until, without any warning, we both ceased.

"My friend," he said to my mother, "your son is not mad. He's just filled with the Holy Spirit."

He took his Bible and flipped to a letter from the Apostle Paul to the church at Corinth. He showed us that one of the ways the Holy Spirit shows himself and encourages believers is through this kind of prayer in a spiritual language. Prayer in this heavenly language gives confidence to the believer that he is praying consistently with the will of God. He does not know what he is saying, but he can be confident it is "in the spirit" and pleasing to God. And along with that confidence, this prayer comes with the joy and peace that always accompany the Holy Spirit.

He continued, "You need to know that it is not given to every believer. See how Paul says, 'To one is given through the Spirit the speaking of wisdom,' to another this, to another that, 'to another various kinds of tongues.' And see, he says that God 'apportions to each one as he wills.' And then 'Do all speak in tongues? Do all prophesy?' He has told us that the answer is no. But it seems to me Jesus has given this holy speech to Swidiq in order to cleanse his mouth from all the evil he's spoken in his life. I don't know, but seems like it to me. The toothbrush, you know, it's for cleaning the mouth."

The truth of his words settled right in to my understanding. How truly my mouth had needed cleansing from all the evil I had said and encouraged! I was momentarily struck with how deeply I had desecrated the gift of my mouth through the years. Not only had I used it for taking drugs and abusing alcohol, but it had been an implement for speaking evil. With my mouth I had led so many people into wickedness, false professions, and commitment to evil that if my mouth was to be made a useful instrument for speaking truth, then truly it needed the toothbrush of Jesus!

After about a month, I was again in my room settling down for the night, when I heard a voice calling, seemingly from a distance, "Swidiq, Swidiq," then a pause, and again, "Swidiq, Swidiq."

I threw off the blanket and opened the door. My mother was in the front room busy with something.

"Did you just call me?" I asked.

"No, did you hear someone?" she said, looking a little worried.

"I was sure I heard someone call me twice. Did you hear anyone out there call my name?"

"I heard nothing. It's a quiet night," she said.

"Never mind," I said, turning back to my room. I knew we were both wondering the same thing. Perhaps I was hearing things that weren't there. Maybe my mind was slipping again. I sat down on the edge of the bed listening intently.

Then it came again, distinctly. "Swidiq, Swidiq," and again, "Swidiq, Swidiq." I am not sure how to explain it, but it came in such a way that I knew it was auditory. It was not a "voice in my head"; it caused my ears to work. I hopped up eagerly this time, expecting to discover someone. I went outside and walked around the house to the external wall of my room. I looked about and studied the ground for any footprints. It was again the rainy season in Rwanda, when the ground remains moist with the daily rains. If someone had stood there, they would have left prints in the mud. There was nothing.

I went back to the room highly puzzled. My suspicions began to turn in the direction of the supernatural, perhaps an angel or jinn or African spirit. I wondered if my allegiance to Jesus had aroused other spirits to seek me out with aims to reclaim me. I came gingerly into the room, determined to listen carefully to the quality of the voice. In death, I had heard the voice of Jesus and the voices of evil spirits; there was definitely a difference.

I sat expectantly on the bed for a few minutes. Once more, the voice vibrated the air, "Swidiq, Swidiq. Swidiq, Swidiq." I was fairly certain this was a good voice, maybe even the voice of Jesus. I was ready to hear, so I sat attentively in the silence. The moments passed. I heard the lowing of a cow nearby. I strained my ear into the quiet of the night. Laughter drifted from a neighbor's house. That was all. Though I sat alert in the silence for another hour, the voice did not speak again.

The next day I sought out pastor Jean-Claude. I had to track him down because he was out visiting, walking the hills to see his people. When I finally found him along the road, I told him about the experience of the night before and about my own speculations. He listened attentively, asking a few questions about my feelings and sensations when I heard the voice. Then he prayed and was stood silent for several minutes.

At last he spoke, "In the Bible, you can read about a man named Samuel who was a prophet of God and leader of his people. When he was small, he did not know the Lord yet, but he slept beside the Tent where

God lived with the people. One night he heard a voice saying, 'Samuel, Samuel.' He thought it was his master, the priest Eli, so he got up to obey. It wasn't Eli. After two more times hearing the voice and going to his master, Eli told him to stay in his place, but if he heard the call again, to say, 'Speak, Lord, your servant is listening.' That's what he did, and it was the Lord. The next time God gave him a message, and from then on he knew the voice of the Lord. I tell you this because God is unchanging. He will do the same kinds of things he has done before so that his people can recognize him. He doesn't trick us or confuse us. He wants us to know him. So go home, and if it comes again, say what Samuel said, 'Speak, Lord. I am listening'" (1 Samuel 3).

I went home wondering what the Lord wanted to tell me. I pondered over the story of Samuel and again marveled at God's everyday dealings with his people. He speaks to people — normal people. I had seen, even that day, how the pastor heard the Lord say something, reminding him of the story of Samuel. Then when he spoke it, the words seemed to put my thoughts in their proper places. Where there was confusion or fear a moment before, the words pushed those things out. Where thoughts were swirling, they became settled. I did not know much about the voice of God, and I did not have confidence that I could recognize its sound, but I was learning its effects. Peace. Order. Rightness. Comfort. When God speaks to someone, or when someone speaks his words, the hearer receives these things. His words put things right.

When I entered my house, almost immediately I heard the voice, "Swidiq, Swidiq," and again, "Swidiq, Swidiq."

"Speak, Lord. I am listening," I said.

With firmness and clarity, the voice of God declared, "You are no longer Swidiq, but a transformed person. You are no longer Swidiq, but a transformed person. You are no longer Swidiq, but a transformed person." Then he was silent.

With each statement of this truth, I felt its re-orienting effects in my mind. God was declaring it, and in the very moment he was saying it, the reality came to be. Like his creating Word that brought order out of chaos at the beginning of creation, or when he said to someone in Galilee, "Be well," his words brought about what they proclaimed. I had known that Jesus is the Lord and that he had saved me, and I knew that he was somehow in me and cleansing me, but as he spoke the words of identity, something changed in the deepest places of my self-understanding. I was no longer Swidiq, but a transformed person, a new man. It was a crucial fact.

Whatever curses had been laid on me, they were undone. Whatever lies I had once believed about myself, they were shown in their falsity. Every lie, every ancestral sin and family curse, every destructive path, and every evil bond that had attached to the name of Swidiq was broken.

That night, I slept with the peace of an infant child in his mother's arms.

Chapter Sixteen

SANCTIFIED IN THE TRUTH

EXPERIENCING THE GREAT JOY and restorative peace of Christ, I wanted to share this new life with others. I knew the striving and anxiety of my Muslim family and friends, and I wanted so much for them to feel the freedom given by the grace of Jesus. I offered myself unreservedly to the Lord and seized every opportunity to tell more people what I had experienced or to share in greater depth with those near me. The Lord is pleased with our willingness to speak of him, so my submission was blessed with many opportunities.

Because of the *muhadhara* proselytizing events, I had become fairly well known as a Muslim apologist and speaker against Christianity, so when news of my conversion to Jesus spread around the Kivu region, churches were encouraged. I began receiving invitations to come tell my testimony of Jesus's love and power, and to tell the story of how I had come to know it. My role as an imam was known, so I didn't need to give much backstory. Without trying to explain things theologically, I would simply relate how the Lord had first used the prayers of his people to heal my mind, and then how Jesus had come to me in my death and brought me back to proclaim him. The point of the message was very simple, really. It was the message that Jesus had spoken to me, which Jesus speaks to all who are willing to hear him: "I died for men, and you are among those I died for. Do not deny it any longer." Being the words of Jesus, those words had power to reveal the truth and to convict people who were denying

Jesus, Christian or Muslim in their own respective ways. And the Holy Spirit did convict. Many Christians told me they were encouraged in their faith and emboldened to proclaim the gospel, and a large number of nominal Christians were actually saved. As is sometimes the case, speaking breeds more speaking, and the more I gave my testimony, the more opportunities came.

I was also learning to discern the voice of God more clearly, which came in a variety of ways. For example, a woman came to visit us at my mother's home. I heard the Lord say, "This person is having challenges with her husband," so I inquired about the marriage and her husband's behavior. Although she was startled, asking, "How did you know?" she shared the challenges. I prayed for her and felt confidently guided in my prayer. When she returned home, her husband was eagerly awaiting her return in order to reconcile. On another occasion, as I was giving my testimony and telling of Jesus to a crowd of about 2,000 people, I heard the Lord say, "There is a woman with heart trouble. Look." Even as I was hearing the voice, I saw a woman in the congregation who seemed significantly larger than all the rest, like an adult looks sitting among small children. I pointed to her, confirmed that she was having heart trouble, and invited her up to receive prayer. When she came to join me, she was just the size of any ordinary woman. There was no dramatic indication at the time, but when I saw her a short time later, she explained that she truly had been healed that day.

During this period, I would also wake with a dream fresh in my mind, and what I dreamed would happen soon after. But the Lord would also use dreams to help me understand his Word. The most important of these clarifying dreams concerned the nature of God himself.

I had developed a conviction that I needed the Word of God. If I knew the Qur'an, how much more did I need the true words of God. So I committed to read the entire Bible, and within that first year of following Jesus I read it three times through. But I kept bumping into the problem of the Trinity, which for Muslims is the Achilles heel of Christianity. In the back of my mind were the Muslim arguments against the equality of Jesus with the Father, along with the claim that Christians were polytheists. For instance, when I read Jesus saying to the rich young ruler, "Why do you call me good? No one is good but God alone," I was confused. He seemed to imply both distinction of nature and quality. As I often did, I went to ask the Anglican pastor, Benimana Jean-Claude, what he thought. Rather than try to solve my theological quandary, he told me to fast and ask the Lord to reveal the truth, then read the Bible again.

I took his advice, fasted and asked the Lord to teach me, and began reading. This time I plowed straight through the Scripture without stopping. I read the Old Testament and had begun the New Testament when I became overwhelmingly exhausted. After the genealogy in Matthew, I fell asleep and immediately into a dream.

I dreamed that President Paul Kigame, the president of Rwanda, was visiting our village like he sometimes visits villages throughout the country. There were many guards securing the area and watching carefully as the President interacted with the people. He paused here and there, chatting with shopkeepers. Then a man in the village, named Theoneste, stumbled towards the President. He had been drinking too much, and he came towards the President shouting out abusive things. The guards surrounded him immediately and took him away. The picture then vanished.

Still asleep, I heard the Lord ask, "Why was this man arrested? Are you sure it was Theoneste who was speaking?"

I answered, "Yes. If you abuse the President, you will be arrested."

"But it was the tongue that spoke. Why not just arrest the tongue?" the Lord said. "It is because you can't separate the voice from the man. It *is* the man. The man cannot be separated from his voice or the breath that makes the man breathe. This also is like God — Father, Son, and Holy Spirit." And then I woke.

While another person might require a different sort of explanation to open up their understanding of the Trinity, this communication from the Lord was exactly what I needed. I came back to the Bible with eagerness and delight, and I finished it joyfully and with comprehension. The whole story of the Bible and the single path for the redemption of humankind seemed to fall into place. With the hindrance removed, the Scriptures filled up my thinking as the Holy Spirit used it to shape how I understood everything. As I took in the Bible, the Lord rewrote my account of the world and the ways of God with man, according to his Word rather than according to Islamic tradition.

The more filled with the Scriptures I became, the more truly and powerfully I could speak of what the Lord had actually done in me. The Bible gave me a vocabulary and the context to understand what Jesus had done. I increasingly understood both what I had been saved from and the glorious inheritance I had been saved into. For evangelistic preaching, an important step was that more and more I was able to connect what the Lord had done specifically in my case with what he always does when he redeems any life. So in light of what the Lord had done for me, I was better able to call listeners to repentance and into the same freedom in which I found myself.

Those who have truly known the Lord for very long also know that being filled with God's Word opened up another avenue of intimate communication with the Lord. We know that the Lord is the same yesterday, today, and forever (Heb. 13:8; Mal. 3:6), and though heaven and earth will pass away, his words will remain (Luke 21:33; Matt. 24:35). In other words, God says what God says, which is essentially the same in every age — always relevant, always fresh, always bringing life. Consequently, the actual words of the Bible are a constant way that he communicates. With the Scriptures filling my mind, I came to count on the Lord to bring a phrase or a passage to mind when a situation called for wisdom or insight. I now understood what was happening so often when I met with Pastor Jean-Claude. The Holy Spirit speaks in us using the very words he had given to the prophets and apostles.

Through the regularity of God's speaking in this way, I learned to pay close attention when a verse or a passage came unsought to my mind. I learned that God was speaking for a specific reason — sometimes to prepare me for a conversation, sometimes for much-needed encouragement or comfort, and sometimes to warn me of upcoming trouble. Of the latter there was a significant share, and I found that there is a time to act on Jesus's words, "When they persecute you in one city, flee to another" (Matt. 10:23).

Chapter Seventeen

BACKLASH

WHENEVER ONE LEAVES A RELIGIOUS COMMUNITY or departs from his family's faith, there is a cost. At the least, the community or family will feel a sense of betrayal, loss, or rejection. If you think of a Christian family who has a child that becomes an atheist, you will see that those feelings are common to people of all faiths. In addition to those universal dynamics, leaving Islam brings an entirely different set of trials, and the stakes are much higher.

I have learned that the view of Islam prevalent in Western nations is confused, which is not surprising because global Islam today is more fraught with division and intra-religious turmoil than has ever been. In addition to the longstanding divisions of Sunni and Shi'ite, there are also Arab and non-Arab factions, tribally based factions, Sufism (a mystical movement that cuts across Sunni and Shi'ite lines), sects like Ahmadiyya and Wahhabi, and splinter groups from the Nation of Islam in North America. Likewise, as I mentioned earlier with reference to my own family's practice, wherever Islam conquered, from its very first inception, it has incorporated religious practices of the conquered nations, resulting in countless varieties of Folk Islam around the world (not to mention the difference between this everyday Folk Islam and the professions of Formal Islam). The rise of so-called fundamentalist Islam, such as the violent organizations like the Taliban, Al Qaeda, Muslim Brotherhood, Al Shabaab, Boko Haram, and most recently the Islamic State, further confuses the picture of Islam as its internal fissures increasingly produce major fractures.[8]

When sorting through the confusion, it is good to consider that Islamic tradition provides different guidance for Muslims on how to live depending on the size of the Muslim presence in a country. Like faithful Christians, Muslims think their religion will one day fill the earth. Unlike Christians, though, who follow Jesus in his insistence that "my kingdom is not of this world" (John 18:36), Muslims must establish this global presence themselves by altering the political, social, economic, educational, and judicial aspects of a society. A minority Islamic community will follow Islamic traditions and exercise *sharia* only to the extent their society and government allow, even if it means only within individual family units. Nevertheless, an organized Islamic community will always press for an extension of those allowances. The larger the Muslim presence, the more insistence on legal guarantees for *sharia*. And with every gain, the Islamic community is emboldened for more intense pressure.

Recent reports suggest that the population of Rwanda today is approximately 14% Muslim, around three times as high as before the 1994 genocide. Muslims in Rwanda are financially supported by Muslim organizations in Saudi Arabia, Sudan, and Pakistan, and they have grown in their social and political influence. At the time I renounced Islam and began proclaiming Jesus, the Muslim population was closer to 6%.

Despite the relatively small number, Rwandan Muslims have attempted to follow Islamic tradition on "apostates," or those who turn from Islam to another faith. The hadith of Islamic tradition are in total agreement that "The Prophet said, 'If somebody [a Muslim] discards his religion, kill him'" (al-Bukhari 52.260), or in the hadith of the 8th Century Imam Malik, "The Messenger of Allah said, 'If someone changes his religion — then strike off his head,' which refers to those who leave Islam" (36.15). In my situation, both my prominence in the local Muslim community, especially as a former apologist in *muhadhara*, and my outspokenness in proclaiming Jesus as Lord, gave them strong reasons to fulfill the dictates of *sharia* regarding an apostate.

Very soon after I had begun to speak in churches about the truth of Jesus, a somewhat nominal Christian I had known for a while asked me

---

8. William J. Saal's *Reaching Muslims for Christ* (Moody, 1991), is an excellent introduction for getting to know Muslim immigrants and speaking with them about the hope of Jesus.

to visit and pray. He prepared some food and then asked me to pray for some concerns. As I left, I felt a little light-headed and pained in the gut. For the next two days, I was having cramps and pains inside. My mother noticed and asked me to breathe out heavily. Somehow, by the smell of my breath, she determined that I had been poisoned. She rushed to get expunging herbs, which caused me to vomit the poisoned contents. Word travels fast in villages, and we soon learned that the Muslim leaders had paid this nominal Christian to lure me under false pretenses and poison me. We have to admit that Christians can have a form of faith and even appearance of godliness, but deny its power (2 Timothy 3:5). The temptation of money can overwhelm whatever convictions were there, especially where poverty is gripping.

A short time later, I took a long boat trip down the whole length of Lake Kivu from Gisenyi to Cyangugu, at the southern tip of the lake. These trips are a rare pleasure. Lake Kivu fills a wide, deep gorge of the Rift Valley between Congo and Rwanda, making it one of the deepest lakes in the world. The terraced hills of Rwanda dive steeply into the lake, while the mountain forests of Congo seem to forbid entrance. Together, they hold the lake in placid calm, making it delightful for boat trips. In the forests on either shore, there are species of birds found nowhere else in the world, and the calm waters invite hundreds of feathered visitors.

Along the journey south, boats put into shore at numerous points for passengers to disembark and for others to take their place. As our boat came into a port, I heard the voice of God say, "Get off the boat." I knew his voice well enough by that time that I was quick to obey. Making my way off the boat with the departing passengers, I noticed a man following me, hurriedly picking his way through the people on the opposite side of the boat. He was not able to reach the gangway before the press of incoming passengers began, so that he was trapped on the boat by the crowd. As the boat departed, I could see him still watching me from the rail. I made my way to Cyangugu by bus and kept my appointments, but when I returned to Gisenyi, it was rumored in the town that the Muslims had missed an opportunity to kill me on the lake.

Notwithstanding these attempts to harm me, the Holy Spirit was giving me greater boldness as I was absorbing the Word and coming to know the Lord Jesus more and more. While Muslims run towards death in *jihad* hoping to secure a guarantee of heaven, I was finding that the Holy Spirit is the deposit of God, the true guarantee of heaven (Eph. 1:14), so that believers in Jesus can walk in perfect confidence, indifferent to death. The Holy Spirit gives joy as you speak the love and mercy of Jesus, so that "to live is Christ, to die is gain" (Phil. 1:21). It was a great kindness of God to give this confidence and boldness because the hatred from my former community — even family and friends — only intensified.

During the next year, as I went on a trip to preach the gospel from Gisenyi to Kibuye and then north to Ruhengeri, I occasionally sensed a restless hostility somewhere in the crowds. On this tour, churches would organize open-air events near town centers and markets. In East Africa (and most of Africa generally) the pace of life is unhurried. With agriculture and animal husbandry as the dominant way of life — very much like the life depicted in the New Testament — people walk slowly, stop and talk with every acquaintance they meet, and rarely have appointments to rush off to. If a group sets up a stage, a speaker, and a microphone in a town center, it is most likely the most interesting thing happening for miles around. Add a drum and some singers, and regardless of who is speaking, people gather. These kinds of gatherings gain in energy and expectance when the speaker is known to have a good story, and the more I preached, the more my story went ahead of me and stirred interest.

During this tour, I came to a town with a significant Muslim community. The drum had called the people together and a choir had sung to continue drawing people to the congregation. I was just standing to speak when there was a disturbance in the crowd. A young man had been slowly shouldering his way forward, when someone spotted a gun tucked inside his jacket. The crowd surrounded him, shouting. They grabbed him and disarmed him, keeping him from escaping. Others called to the police, who are often nearby when there are large gatherings. After they had arrested him, he confessed that Muslims in the area had given him 20,000RWF (today about $25) to kill me.

Back home in Gisenyi, I went to give an evening message at a nearby parish. I had been away for some time, and it was known around town that I would be addressing the deceptions of Islam that evening. It was a crowded church, and the Spirit of the Lord was at work, taking truth and using it to bring clarity to many who had not been clear about the stark differences between Christianity and Islam. Everyone there had acquaintances or family members who had become Muslim, so the subject hit close to home. That night I told some of the ways that I, when an imam, had attempted to conceal facets of Islam and to undermine the faith of Christians. I explained, too, the methods Muslims typically use to convert Christians, and I returned again and again to the steadfast and everlasting grace that comes through Jesus Christ, and our dependence on the Holy Spirit for the work of conviction and conversion. What I did not know is that the Muslims had decided this would be my last message in Gisenyi.

The meeting went long, so that when I returned it was very dark. As anywhere in the developing world, the expense of electricity and relatively few exterior lights on homes means a walk after dark is slow going, and a night with a new moon is especially black. Where we know the road is rough, we often use the light on our cell phone to keep us from falling into holes. I picked my way from one side of town towards the town center, which I would pass through on the way to my home on the other side of town. As I came into the brighter area around the shops, I heard God or his messenger say, "Don't go home. Stay here." So I sat down on a curb and waited, listening. Out of the corner of my eye, I saw a movement in the shadows at the end of the row of shops, just where the glow from the shop lights failed to reach. Looking peripherally to those shadows, I could see several men watching me, right along the road towards my home. Even a few months before this, I would have considered going towards them to challenge them in fight, but the work of the Spirit had been thorough in me. I still waited, listening for the Lord.

After about an hour, I no longer saw anyone lingering in the shadows. I stood up, deciding that it was safe to continue my journey home. I took a few steps in that direction, and the Voice said, "No, go back to where you preached and stay there." This was all the instruction I needed, so I turned on my heels and picked my way back along the darkened road. I returned to the church and spent the night at the pastor's home. In the morning I again came to the town center on my way home. I ran into a few friends from the church, and they said that a man had been attacked last night passing along the road from the town. In the darkness, his attackers had beat him almost to death, until they realized they had attacked the wrong person.

It may be tempting to rationalize these attempts to kill me as a unique local issue, maybe tied up with personal vindictiveness or just part of African practice. I only wish that were the case. Despite all its varieties and regional particularities of emphasis, Islam has always embraced and legally enshrined death for those who leave the House of Islam. Sharia is to Islam what the gospel is to Christianity — the essential expression of the faith and therefore inseparable from the religion. Where sharia is not fully practiced, the restraint is due to the non-Muslim political and legal system, as well as to international economic and political pressure, not due to the preference of the Muslim leaders. Wherever Islam has official sanction for sharia, its faithful will move to punish apostates with death, but especially those apostates who have held places of honor or leadership. It is simply part of being a Muslim community obedient to the Qur'an and the traditions of Muhammad.

Chapter Eighteen

JESUS IS STRONGER

DURING THE FIRST TWO YEARS after Jesus had awakened me and sent me to proclaim him, opposition to the gospel was not confined to the Muslim community. My stepmother had bitterly resented the honor I had received as an imam, but even more her hatred was aroused by the work of Jesus in me. When others spoke well of me, she spat out curses, and if I greeted her in the marketplace with kindness and goodwill, she remained silent with eyes burning with hate. Her deep animosity in my childhood had never made rational sense, but now, fueled by a malice from the realms of evil, she determined to use all the resources of darkness to stop me from flourishing.

Even as the mosque leaders were making efforts to destroy me, she attempted to use charms and curses against me. Whenever she knew of a planned attack, she would work her own sorcery and try to blind me to the attack. But no matter what efforts she made to weaken, confuse, or blind me, the light of the Lord and his irresistible Voice pierced every darkness and kept me from harm.

But there is a kind of hierarchy of sorcery, and failing to attain her ends, my stepmother sought out a sorcerer known to have greater powers. Some witches communicate more directly with demonic forces, who are the ones actually having the power and who hold the witch in slavery. To outside observers, it appears that the witch has the power. My stepmother went to one such sorcerer.

In the process of crafting curses and charms, sorcerers ask their client to steal some possession from the person to be cursed — an item of clothing, jewelry, or personal tool. They take the item and place it on a mirror. As the item sits on the divining mirror, demons respond and bring the face of the person to be cursed. This image in the mirror indicates to the sorcerer that the spirits have a foothold with the person — some way that the person has yielded an entry to evil so that the demon may get power over them — and that the curse will be effective. From her gossip, my stepmother told others that she had sought a witch who used these methods, but the witches were unable to curse me because the spirits could not bring my image to the mirror. Regardless of different items she brought, the demons were not able to claim any kind of control over me. My stepmother's conclusion was that I had a stronger witch working for me, or that I myself was using stronger witchcraft. Her mind was so darkened that she could not even consider the truth: Jesus is stronger than every power (Eph. 1:20-22).

My mother, though, who had confessed Jesus on the day of my rising and had joined fellowship with the Church, was suffering greatly from spiritual attacks. At times, even as she walked along the road, she would be demonically oppressed to the point of being physically restrained. She would be clutched or thrown down in the middle of the road. From the time of beginning to preach and have active ministry in the church, I had been living with some other Christians of the church who wanted to support this work. But in view of her struggles, I decided to return to my mother's house in order to take forty days to fast and pray for her. By joining her household again, I wanted to wage spiritual battle against the evil that was oppressing her.

Towards the end of the forty days, I dreamed of a man coming to the garden inside the boundary hedges of the house. He went to a certain spot in the corner of the garden and lifted three stones with writing on them. In the dream, I was fully aware that these three stones represented my mother, my father, and me. Then I woke.

Immediately, I jumped up, grabbed a spade, and went to the spot in the garden that I had seen in the dream. I dug and soon found three stones bound with a cord around a small bone, like a chicken bone, along with a pair of my mother's knickers. This kind of binding of objects to an unclean thing connected with death, usually a bone, is a common curse totem. I removed them and threw them in the fire. For three days my hands burned and ached with pain, simply from touching these items used for evil. With the items of cursing removed, I felt the Lord's urging to lead my mother through renunciation of her past occult practices. In place of each evil practice, she made strong professions of truth and of Jesus's rule in that part of life. The power of the oppression was broken.

When a Christian has given place to sin in their lives, or there is some kind of ground Satan can claim, such curses can bring considerable problems to believers. Demonic powers bring oppression based on the sin, like a kind of invitation or open door. The curses of witches and sorcerers just empower demons with malice. But Christians must remember that if a man or woman is in Christ, the blood of Jesus cleanses them from all unrighteousness, and they are, in fact, seated with Christ in the heavenly realms (1 John 1:7-9; Eph. 2:6). They must confess the sin and cancel the ground that the enemy is claiming. Their life is safe — it is hidden with Christ in God (Col. 3:3). Jesus is stronger, and no weapon formed against us can prosper when "neither death, nor life, nor angels, nor rulers, nor powers, nor things present, nor things to come, nor height, nor depth, nor any other creature will be able to separate us from the love of God in Christ Jesus our Lord" (Romans 8:38-39).

As I mentioned, my dream revealed that one of the stones was for my father. On the day of my awakening from death, he had been shocked along with everyone else. Throughout my illness, he had been the one who had taken me to the doctors and sought every means for health. He had heard firsthand that there had been no hope, and then he had seen the promised death come about. My rising and immediate confession of Jesus were as much disconcerting to him as they were terrifying. Within moments, as he heard the name of Jesus on my lips, my father knew that things would never be the same. As a sheikh, what might have been an honor to him — a son returning from death — became a horrible shame when I proclaimed Jesus as Lord. He was torn — his son was well but was instantly no longer a son he could claim. In the back of his mind, though, he stored away the facts.

Initially, the whole Muslim community hoped that I had been delusional and would return to confessing Allah. But after I had visited Faraji with my atypical evangelism, and when it was clear that I was joining in fellowship with the Christians, the elders of the mosque all agreed that my father must force my return. The mosque was shamed, Islam was shamed, but most of all my father was shamed. It was too much for him. He announced publicly that if he found me at home, he would kill me. It was about that time that I shifted away from staying with either of my parents and moved in with the Christian friends. In the heat of his anger, my father went to their house, shouting curses and threatening them.

In his shame and anger, my father met with the *jamaat*, the mature males of the mosque. At this meeting they determined that I was irrecoverable for Islam and a true apostate, so it was the beginning of their attempts on my life. Desiring to cover his shame, my father took the initiative to plan the first attack. Their plan was that my father would send me word to come to his house to reconcile. When I came, others would be ready.

When the day arrived, I was glad to hear that my father wanted to talk and restore our relationship. I was planning to keep the appointment until I ran into a woman along the road. In rural places, Rwandans greet everyone they pass with various greetings appropriate to the social relationship. As I was soon to pass a woman balancing a big bag of rice on her head, I first noted that she was a Muslim because she wore a *hijab*, the head covering with a scarf that covers the neck. When she was closer, I realized that this was a woman whom I knew to be secretly a Christian.

We slowed to make customary greetings, but she said quickly and quietly, "Don't go to your father's house. It's his trick. They plan to kill you," and then concluded loudly, "*Amakuru ni meza*" (like "I'm doing well"), pretending I had greeted her. "He's in the town," she said, then continued on her way, not waiting for a reply.

I took her warning seriously and went a long way around to approach my father's house from the back. As I crept up behind a bush near the house, I saw two men wearing Muslim *kufi* caps working their way through the large bushes beside the house and moving to a vantage point to watch the road. I could see that each of them carried machetes. They crouched in the bush, waiting for me to come along at the expected time. I slipped silently away and returned to the town center the way I had come.

I moved quickly from shop to shop, looking for my father. I spotted him standing with one of his old friends. As I walked towards him, they looked up and were visibly startled to see me. His face contorted, trying to find a shape that seemed confident; he failed in the attempt and settled for anxiously haughty. His friend slipped away, sensing a confrontation.

Ignoring the niceties, I came directly to the point. "Why do you want to kill me?" I said, gesturing to him with an open hand.

He folded his arms. "You are out of your mind, I think. Who is trying to kill you?" he said.

"You and I both know that there are two men hidden outside your house right now. And they're not cutting crops with those machetes. You're supposed to be meeting me there. And yet, here you are."

"I was soon to come," he said. "I stopped to greet *akhi* (my Muslim brother) as I was coming. You know, a guest is always prisoner of the host."

Despite his denials, I felt the peace of the Lord fill me and calm me. As I looked at him, he seemed almost to change before my eyes. Although he is a head taller than me, I saw him as small and afraid.

With perfect calm and softness, I said, "My father, you should remember that the night has ears. I know that you arranged to have me killed today, but I want you to know that I love you." I turned and walked towards the church.

In the days that followed, as the Muslims made the attempts on my life that I described earlier, my father began wondering, "What kind of God is this who reveals secrets? What kind of God takes such trouble for one person?" Like Gamaliel when the Sanhedrin debated about the apostles preaching in Jerusalem, he began wondering if attacking me might be opposing the will of Allah. At the very least, it seemed that the attacks were fruitless and further embarrassing to Islam. Through these reflections, his anger calmed.

One night he sat alone and began reviewing his life. He thought of how he had abandoned his children to suffering, leaving them defenseless. He recalled how he had consented to his second wife's use of witchcraft against his own son time and again, but also how it had been defeated by Jesus. And he considered more recent days, when his wife's enchantments had been unable even to hinder his son's preaching. He concluded that there must truly be a power protecting me, and that power was too great to be opposed. When all was said and done, I had been resurrected. And he reflected that death cannot be overcome without the power of Allah himself.

After Friday prayers, he called together the elders of the mosque and shared his conclusions. He recalled how he had been among the first to embrace Islam, and how he had been blessed with wealth and had poured it back to the honor of Allah. He gestured to the mosque in which they were meeting. He acknowledged that the shame of my apostasy was chiefly his, as the father and the sheikh, but he had come to the conclusion that Allah must want me to be alive. At the least, he reasoned, Allah had given my life into the hands of some mighty Power. Death could not be defeated without Allah's permission. And time after time some Power had warned me and kept me safe despite their best attempts. He said that he was not sure why Allah would consent to my protection, but he had come to believe that they might be opposing Allah in trying to kill me. He was sure they would not succeed, so they might as well stop the efforts that only brought more shame.

Although he reasoned entirely from the perspective of an East African Muslim, it was an opening. He had seen an important truth. When Jesus had decided something, it could not be successfully opposed. And when Jesus opens a door, no one can shut it (Rev. 3:7).

Chapter Nineteen

WELCOMING THE STRANGER

AROUND THE TIME MY FATHER MET with the jamaat to call off the attempts to kill me, I decided that it was time to leave Gisenyi for Kigali. My father seemed to be genuinely warming towards me, and I wanted to do whatever I could to make things easier on our relationship and to ease the pressures on him. I figured that he would get some relief if my presence were not a constant reminder of his shame. Admittedly, another part of me was simply tired of dealing with the steady antagonism from my former community. While I was not shaking the dust from my feet against Gisenyi, I was ready for a season of less hostility. In retrospect, I needed some rest.

I went to Kigali, to a parish in the area called Remera. It was the rainy season when I came to Kigali, and I spent a few days trudging through the muddy streets looking for a room or apartment to rent. But Kigali has been in a mode of steady growth for the last fifteen years, and even in tough areas like Remera, open living spaces are rare and do not go for cheap. Each night, after a day of fruitless searching, I would sleep at a cheap guesthouse, praying that the Lord would open something the next day.

When Sunday arrived, I went joyfully to the Anglican church. As I came to learn later, Remera is a difficult place for the Church. During the colonial period, the Belgians did not allow their Rwandan domestic workers to live or sell in the European areas of the town. Remera was just on the edge of the European area, so it was the first stop for workers returning at the end of the day. In those days it filled with places for drink, sex, and trade in stolen goods. Consequently, it won a reputation for sin and debauchery, and even decades later it carried the spiritual atmosphere of a place claimed by evil. Today it is known to have Kigali's "red light district," along with many bars and crime. In a more hidden layer of society not obvious to foreign visitors, if someone is looking for a witch or medium, they will also find them in Remera. This spiritual situation makes life challenging for the Church. On one hand, the faithful Christians depend on one another for support. On the other hand, the wicked surroundings can cause people to be suspicious of newcomers.

During the worship, the rain poured down on the metal roof and ran in rivers down the streets. For churches in the city, the rainy season has the salutary effect of keeping people together for longer than they might otherwise stay. Whereas rural parishes come together for morning worship that runs long into the afternoon, often five or six hours, with people drifting in and out to eat if they can, churches in the city are more affected by Western thinking about time and attention. Outside the city, the church gathering is by far the best thing happening in the area, but in the city the church has competition for peoples' attention. In the rainy season, though, the downpours deter a hasty exit and encourage longer times of worship and fellowship.

Once the worship had ended, I chatted with those around me, hoping that someone might know of a place to live. Pushing past the reserve that had become common for the people in Remera, a man came forward and introduced himself as Edward, a school teacher. He recognized me from a conference. In Rwanda, a conference is what we call a series of church gatherings over a few days with invited speakers for encouragement, discipleship, and evangelism. I had shared my testimony at that conference, and Edward was very glad to welcome me to the church. When I told him of my struggles to find housing, he quickly invited me to come to his house to stay with his family.

I lived with Edward's family in the Remera Parish of Kigali for three years. At first, aside from Edward's family I detected some hesitance towards me in the Remera church. Picking up on some hints, Edward suggested that there was some fear due to my Muslim background. In a place like Remera, where the Enemy so frequently uses fear and suspicion against the Church, Christians were giving in to fear that perhaps I would bring danger on the parish. They worried that if they identified with me, helped me, and encouraged me, then Muslims in the city would become violent towards them. Some even worried that I might somehow revert back to Islam and then harm them. Fear is a strange thing and often irrational, but it can quickly make people forget some of the most basic commandments of God, like "love your neighbor as yourself" (Luke 10:27) and "welcome the stranger, for you were strangers in the land of Egypt" (Deut. 10:19). But fear is also a thing easily forgiven because we have all felt it and have all given in to it from time to time.

This is perhaps a timely reminder for Christians throughout the world, but especially in areas where global migrations are bringing foreigners into new countries by the thousands. Most obviously, intra-Islamic strife is displacing thousands from Syria, Afghanistan, Iraq, and Sudan. In times like these, the Enemy of souls seeks to stir up fear so that Christians will deny the power of God and will fail to share the love of Jesus. It is crucial that Christians remember that Jesus is the Sovereign Lord and the Owner of all things. Every nation belongs to him, and he will work all things according to the counsel of his own will (Eph. 1:11). For their own behavior, though, Christians must recall the truth that others will know they are true disciples of Jesus by their love, and a willingness to welcome the stranger with care and hospitality will not only work against one's own fears but will soften the hearts of the vulnerable immigrant. "We love because he first loved us" (1 John 4:19), but the one who loves little shows that he has forgotten the forgiveness of his own sins (Luke 7:47). When a person is in love with the things of the world, then he clutches and grasps his possessions, his privileges, his comforts and his status as if they belonged to him by right. That posture plays into the hand of the Enemy and chokes out the love of God.

Eventually, my brothers and sisters in Kigali did warm to me, and I found a home in the Kigali Diocese. Because I had been known as a Rasta artist in some parts of Kigali, the news of my conversion again opened many opportunities to speak and preach. Here, the news was not that the young imam had converted, but that the drug-pushing Rasta dancer had come to Jesus. Still, my message was the same: Jesus is Lord and he wants your life — he wants your whole life without reservation. Invitations to speak came from parishes all over the city. And since people from around the country come to Kigali for the yearly conferences, those events brought steady opportunities for me to speak about the glory of Jesus and his surprising works of redemption.

These speaking engagements brought me into connection with Christians across denominations, but especially with Pentecostals. During the period of restoration since the genocide, Pentecostal churches have sprung up and flourished throughout Rwanda. Unlike the Catholic and Anglican Churches, they had no institutional baggage from the pre-genocide era. They could claim a clean slate and offer a new start as brand new worshiping communities. Moreover, the vigorous praise and the message of the Pentecostal churches — of prosperity and health for faithfulness — have been very attractive to Africans who struggle with poverty and pain.

In many ways, I resonated with the Pentecostals I encountered. They were serious about the power of Jesus to change lives and work in dramatic ways. They prayed for healing and expected it. They were passionate. When I preached in their churches, there was always dramatic response. Church members and visitors sought prayer and desired to live in the power of Christ. Notwithstanding these encouragements, a few interactions with a couple of Pentecostal pastors left me confused.

"You haven't been water baptized?" the pastor of a large Pentecostal church asked one day, when the subject of baptism by the Holy Spirit came up. "What are those Anglicans teaching you?"

"I think everyone just assumed that it had been done already. Since my conversion I've moved around a lot," I said, a little taken aback by the criticism.

"It's one of the problems with the old churches. They do it for babies and then forget everyone else. See what happens with all those babies that are baptized. They grow up thinking they're saved but they don't have the Spirit. If only they would wait, then they would know they're saved and their baptism would mean something. And the way matters, too. When your Anglicans do it, they do it wrong. Jesus was baptized in a river. If it's not fully in the water, it's not real baptism. The Holy Spirit came on Jesus after he came up out of the water. That's the sign of blessing for his action. Just look around you. Anglicans aren't saved."

"What about Paul? After his conversion he was baptized by Ananias. Seems like in the house. Or Cornelius and his household with Peter? Or the Philippian jailer? Acts says 'he was baptized at once with his family' —

in the middle of the night at their house," I said.

He was indignant. "It was under the water and everyone was old enough to believe. If it doesn't say otherwise, then you have to go with the ones that are described. John the Baptist, Jesus, Philip with the Ethiopian. *We* read what the Bible says, not what it doesn't say," he said.

I decided to let the conversation go, but I was confused. This was not the first time that a Pentecostal had told me Anglicans are not saved. Yes, there was obviously more energy in the Pentecostal worship. There was more dance, more time for powerful prayer, more emotion. People could be more African in their worship. And he was right that lots of Catholics and Anglicans and Presbyterians grew up in the church and never seemed to know Jesus and love him. Of course, I had also seen that Pentecostals had their own versions of nominalism and hypocrisy. That was part of the reason I frequently preached to Christians — believers in every denomination needed to know and love the Jesus who has saved them. But was he right that Anglicans aren't saved? That baptism could be part of the common problem of nominalism?

As I had done in the past, I decided to commit the problem to the Lord and take some time to seek his wisdom. The Pentecostals seemed to have strong views on everything, while the Anglicans were much looser on things. Anglicans consigned a lot to "matters indifferent." I realized that I needed a little more time for discipleship. I decided to tackle the issue of baptism first. I took time to read and re-read all the relevant passages, asking the Lord for understanding. After praying one day, I dozed with my Bible open in my hands. Somewhere between sleeping and waking, I heard a Voice whispering, "Read John 3." I woke fully and flipped to the passage. I had read it many times before, but as I read in obedience, my attention was captured by Jesus's words "water and the spirit." I felt with certainty that water baptism was necessary, but the question remained open about the right method. I knew what the Pentecostals thought, so I figured it was time to hear what my own church taught.

The next day I went to meet the pastor of the Remera Parish, Peter Twahirwa, who was a Canon, or designated teacher of the church. I shared with him my conversation with the Pentecostal pastor and my confusion about the different methods.

After listening, he said, "Yes, you have discovered a difference between the churches. Each Pentecostal church takes a position on a matter. They have to defend it strongly because it is part of what makes their church different from all the others, especially us older churches. And since they don't have to be accountable to any other church, they can make every matter an essential one. On the upside, it helps them preach boldly and confidently. On the downside, they can think everyone else is not saved."

"So why do we not use baptism of immersion, like Jesus did?" I asked.

"We do!" he said with a smile. "You were right in what you said to him. The Bible doesn't command any specific method, but it suggests several. John the Baptist and Philip baptized adults at the river, and then the whole family of Cornelius and the family of the Philippian jailer were baptized. At least the jailer was at night in his house. What the Bible doesn't command explicitly, we let the historical practice of the church determine. Basically, it depends on how much water is around!"

"We could do immersion here, then?"

"We can do sprinkling, or three pours in the name of the Father, Son, and Holy Spirit, or immersion. They're all allowed by the church because they're all part of the Church's practice through the years. What's important for an adult is that they need to ask for baptism. When children are part of a Christian family, they are baptized into the faith in which they will be raised and taught, like Jewish boys circumcised on the eighth day. There will never be a time when they don't know Jesus is Lord. They're Christians and we don't want to pretend they have to have complete understanding of doctrine before they can know him. What we say is that in baptism, God is the one doing the action — he is the one adopting the person. It's a sign of what he has done in bringing the person into the family of Jesus. At Confirmation is when they will declare their decision to continue in the Christian family where God has placed them."

"So, are you saying that since I'm an adult I need to be both baptized and confirmed. Is that right? I've been adopted, and I need to confirm my decision to be in the church," I said.

"That's right. You become confirmed as part of God's Church, and the bishop blesses you to serve in it. To be a missionary for his kingdom wherever you live. Since you're serving already, the sooner the better," he said.

"I'd like to be immersed, if I can. I don't want the Pentecostals to doubt my baptism, and I want to be able to preach with them, too."

"Yes, we can do that," he said. "Just be sure that the method of baptism doesn't determine salvation in your mind. I want you to remember all those Anglican brothers who helped you know Jesus and his love in Gisenyi. Remember Pastor Jean-Claude and your friends. Most of them had water poured on their heads as babies."

With a surprise of kindness from the Lord, when Canon Twahirwa gave the date for my baptism, it was February 28, both my birthday and the date of my return from death. When the day came and I submitted to the baptism, I felt a distinct touch of the Holy Spirit's power. The joy of the Lord surged through me, doing the mysterious work of grace, assuring me of my adoption as a son. At the same time, the Spirit drove out a fear I had carried — a tendency to worry about what was going to happen in my life. Somehow, through that baptism, I became certain that my Father would guide me every step of the way because I am his son.

In keeping with that celebration of adoption, I chose a new name. I remembered when the Voice of God had said, "You are no longer Swidiq, but a transformed person," so I wanted to acknowledge that change in my name. I chose the name Cedric, which was close to Swidiq and had been the name of an honorable boy at my secondary school. He had lived the kind of upright and honorable life I now wanted to live. So when the immersion came, the pastor said, "I baptize you, Cedric Kanana, in the name of the Father, and of the Son, and of the Holy Spirit."

When Confirmation came around, I was confident to claim my place in the Church and to receive a blessing from Archbishop Emmanuel Kolini to minister in the Anglican Church of Rwanda. It would be dishonest to say that I never again questioned Anglican ways of worship or practicing ministry, but since then I have been committed to working things out from within.

After three years in Kigali living with Edward's family and serving as parish secretary for a new parish, I felt drawn back home to Kivu to preach the gospel. Having wise foresight, leaders in the church urged me to seek theological education to prepare for ordained ministry, but all I wanted to do was evangelize. Nothing gave me more joy and pleasure than telling the greatness of Jesus and his real willingness to save any who will look to him and call on his name. So I put off further education for the time being and went zealously back to Kivu for public proclamation of the saving work of Jesus. At the invitation of Bishop John Rucyahana, I joined the Shyira Diocese as a leader of intercessors, and shortly thereafter as leader of youth work in the diocese. But always my heart was burning to proclaim the gospel, and I leapt at every opportunity, whether it was speaking to Christians or Muslims, old or young, within churches or out in the public arena.

Chapter Twenty

TURNING THEIR HEARTS BACK AGAIN

ONE OF THE GREATEST BLESSINGS of my return to Kivu was to be back near my father during what became a trying time for him. He had married my step-mother back in 1995 partly to avenge himself on my mother's Tutsi family and partly to satisfy the insistence from his Hutu family. Not only was this decision born from evil considerations, the match itself was fraught with conflict. "There is a way that seems right to a man, but in the end it leads to death" (Prov. 16:25).

My father's quiet and reflective demeanor mixed badly with the strong will and manipulative character of his second wife. And as I have told already, he always suspected that she used sorcery and witchcraft to influence him. Things became much worse after my conversion, though. At first, she applied witchcraft to join in his attempts to bring me back to submission to Islam. But when he recognized that no power could overcome Jesus and eventually came to terms with the shame caused by my conversion, her hatred towards me became hotter and her antagonism towards him increased in proportion.

In small communities, no one can hide domestic troubles. We say "the night has ears," but partly what we mean is that in the stillness of the night, the whole neighborhood can hear the arguments in your house. So villages love gossip like a tasty treat. My stepmother's belligerence in the home became a topic of public conversation — and an additional source of shame for my father. Adding to the shame, his wife felt threatened by the gossip, and she began using witchcraft unabashedly to cause him physical pains. You can imagine the bind he was in. His home was in turmoil, but he could not go to other Muslims for help with her, as that in itself would compound the shame for failing to control his wife. Although he wanted to escape the marriage, he feared her use of evil powers. It was about this time that I returned to Kivu.

During my previous visits home over the last three years, my father had jokingly called me "the pastor," but in reality, there was some kind of belief in his words. As he found himself caught between domestic misery and public shame, he confided his struggle to me. Remarkably, despite his Muslim faith, he wanted prayer and was willing to receive prayers in the name of Jesus Christ. He acknowledged the fact that Jesus's name was powerful. Through this prayer, he received temporary relief from the physical pain, but what is more, he grew in understanding that the power of Jesus is universal, not just confined to the space of the church or applicable only to those who are Christians. It was a timely discovery.

In 2012, Rwanda's Islamic community went through a time of internal upheaval due to increasing tensions in the Sunni-Shia divide globally. Up to that time, Rwandan Muslims were both Sunni and Shia, depending largely on the source of funding for the mosque and the place of education for the converts. By far, though, the majority identified with Sunni Islam. With internal tensions and confusions in Islam made manifest by the so-called Arab Spring, local Muslim communities around the world found themselves confronting their own internal problems. For many of these communities, including those in Rwanda, the Sunni-Shia divide became grounds for nursing grievances and gave opportunity for scapegoating. Across Rwanda, Shia Muslims were expelled from mosques and denied participation in the *jamaat*. Many moved to Kigali in 2012 and joined a new Shia mosque and community center.

In the mosques of Gisenyi, the shame and anger at my apostasy had not died but only quieted. And while my father had reconciled himself to the situation, most in his mosque had not. Without his knowledge, the *jamaat* of his mosque met and arrived at a decision: he may be a sheikh and a founder of Islam in Rwanda, but his family is an endless source of shame; he must be treated as a Shia and expelled from the mosque. A few days later, at a meeting for the beginning of Ramadan, they accused him of being a Shia and excluded him from the mosque — the very mosque that he had built.

By that time, I had taken a position as Diocesan Secretary in the newly formed Diocese of Kivu. In the Anglican Church, a diocese is a geographical area, and all the churches within that area are under the authority of a bishop (overseer). As more churches are planted, existing dioceses can be divided to form new ones, so that proper spiritual care can be provided. The first bishop of the Diocese of Kivu, Bishop Augustine Ahimana, was a friend from Shyira Diocese, and he invited me to serve in this new diocese that covered the land of my upbringing and was based in my hometown of Gisenyi.

When I heard the news of my father's expulsion, I made a visit to his house. To my great surprise, I found him eating a meal in the middle of the day (and a big one by Rwandan standards, which means it included meat) — during the fast of Ramadan. I guess my surprise showed on my face because I didn't even need to comment to get an explanation.

"The rain falls on everyone, but one gets wetter than the rest," he said, continuing to eat as I came inside and sat down.

"You sound bitter," I replied. "Are you angry?"

He raised his brows in acknowledgment, but then set down the stringy chicken bones he was gnawing, as if he intended to speak. But he sat still, contemplating what to say. I just watched him, giving him space to think.

At last he went on. "You know the proverb, 'He hides that he hates me; I hide that I know it'? I guess I hid the truth from myself, too. I underestimated. I never thought about their envy and resentment. Towards you, yes, but not towards me. I guess, you know, the snakes come out on a sunny day."

"You were surprised, eh? So are you angry, or more like sad?"

"Like I said, the rain, you know. I'm always the one who gets wet. I laid the bricks of that mosque. The land was mine. And all the years." His words faded. After a moment, though, he picked up the chicken again. "But they're fools. It makes no sense! Why fast in the season when there is food?" he said, waving the chicken. "We'll have hunger soon enough and everyone will fast. They just pretend to be righteous."

"You're done with them, then. All of them? Done with Islam?" I asked.

"No, no, Islam is true. These Gisenyi Muslims are just fools. I don't know yet what to do. At least, I can say they have opened some new paths for me."

I wondered what he meant, but I didn't feel a freedom in the Holy Spirit to press the point just then. I knew that I would be nearby and would follow up when the Spirit gave a sense of ease. So each time I came to visit my father, I would come prepared to raise one or two topics from the Qur'an. Although he had been one of the first Rwandan Muslims and had risen in status through his wealth, he was not very well versed in the Qur'an. His position was honorific, not due to knowledge. My purpose was simply to show him what the Qur'an truly teaches. I prayed that the Holy Spirit would very simply allow him to see what is true about God, the world, and how we can know God. Because of his rough treatment at the hands of the *jamaat*, and his bitter wife now eager to separate from him, I knew he was open to looking critically at Islam for perhaps the first time.

His lack of Qur'anic knowledge is true of many Muslims, especially in non-Arab countries. Those who have not learned to read and comprehend Arabic are not able to understand the Qur'an, so they are dependent on their imams, muftis, and sheikhs for explanations of its contents. And just as the imams withhold details from Christians during their attempts to gain converts, they also withhold clear and thorough explanations from the average Muslim. Thus, the dark details of Islam are shrouded by the call to submission and the demand for humble obedience.

After a number of visits, I prepared to bring up a passage from the Qur'an in which Allah gives allowances for Muslims to worship the three daughters of Allah. These three moon goddesses, Al-Lat, Al-Uzza, and Manat, were part of the pagan polytheism of Muhammad's own tribe, for whom Allah was highest among the gods. Their worship had long been linked with the area around the *Ka'aba* in Mecca, which became the holy house of Allah to which all Muslims must attempt pilgrimage. Despite his push for monotheism, Muhammad had initially allowed worship of the moon goddesses, writing them into the Qur'an in one of his visions of the heavenly realms. This allowance helped win the polytheistic tribes around Mecca to his cause. Once he had gained control of the Meccans, he later retracted those verses by claiming they were given by Satan. Nevertheless, like a tantalizing hint to what used to be there, the three goddesses remain in Surah 53, in one of Muhammad's glimpses of Paradise, even though the "Satanic verses" have been removed.[9]

When I brought up the passage and told him about the moon goddesses in the Qur'an, my father was very annoyed. At first he argued about how Christians were twisting the meaning, but when I showed him the passage in his own Qur'an, he just stared, silent, at the text. Despite doubting his own grasp of the spiritual meaning of the Arabic, he could read the text well enough. He knew the passage as one setting up Muhammad's ascent to Paradise with Jibril (Gabriel), and he could see the names of the three goddesses appearing where he would not expect to find other deities. He took up his French translation to verify what he was reading. When he continued to stare at the pages without reengaging our conversation, reading and re-reading, I left shortly.

After about a week, my phone rang and I saw my father's name. After customary greetings, he cut fairly quickly to his purpose. "I see that you are right. I have been in darkness, and Islam is a cloud of darkness. Keep praying for me. I want to know what's true."

When I ended the call, I felt a calm assurance that the Lord had granted my prayers. I was confident that just as Jesus had broken my bonds and freed me to worship him, he was going to free my father too. When we see the movements of the Lord's work, we are emboldened to pray with greater eagerness. We want to see the work accomplished! So as I saw light breaking through the darkness in which my father lived, I prayed all the more that he would come to a full knowledge of the Lord Jesus.

Over the next year, discussion was more difficult because I finally accepted the need for further theological training. I went to Bishop Barham University College in Kabale, Uganda, the Anglican university which was founded as a result of the East African Revival at one of the sites most strongly associated with the revival movement. On the few occasions when I was able to return to Gisenyi, my father and I continued to discuss the Word of God, and each time I could see that he was coming to understand Jesus more and more, and the truth of salvation was not far. As the light of Christ came increasingly into his home, his sorceress wife could not continue in the same house with him. She left with curses on her lips.

---

9. For a literal translation alongside the Arabic, see quran.com.

Turning Their Hearts Back Again

During my studies at Bishop Barham, I met a fascinating woman named Dorcus, who was the granddaughter of Yosiya Kinuka, one of the young Ugandan leaders of the East African Revival who went out in pairs proclaiming Jesus throughout the villages of Rwanda and Uganda. He had been a medical assistant at the Gahini Hospital in Rwanda where the Revival began, and he came with Dr. Joe Church to Kabale, bringing translations of the Bible and the joyful preaching of "walking in the light." This granddaughter of his seemed to be carrying on the family devotion to Jesus, as she was a powerful woman of prayer (not to mention beautiful and brilliant). Prayer and ministry together turned into love, and we were married in December of 2014.

When I took Dorcus home to the village in Kivu, the brothers and sisters of the church gathered for a feast to welcome her into the family. At this gathering, my father stood up among the people to make a speech. After happily welcoming Dorcus to his family and thanking all the guests for their presence, he turned the subject with a tone of grave seriousness in his voice.

"Most of you know me as a Muslim and a founder of Islam here. After 2004, when Cedric passed through death and back to life, I started to see something new. I gave more care to my thoughts and began to look at what I believed. I realized that I wanted my belief to match the truth of what is." He paused for a moment, letting the words sink in and measuring his own. He then continued, "I want to say to all of you that from now on, I follow the God of my son. I know that Jesus is God."

There was stunned silence in the gathering, as the weight of this announcement fell on all our ears. Now he was smiling. "And with this, I want to do right. I want to return to my first wife and seek her forgiveness. And if she is willing, I want to marry her in the church and be right before God."

With such a bold proclamation, I knew he had thought long and hard about this decision. My heart thrilled with the joy of the Holy Spirit, as the reality of his public profession struck home. I could also feel the joy swelling in our gathering as smiles and laughter were breaking out all around. Most of those gathered had no idea that he had been working through the teaching of Islam and the Bible. An impossible thing had just happened: the first Muslim sheikh of Kivu had surrendered to Jesus.

Dying in Islam, Rising in Christ

Of course, I knew that it had taken months and months, even years, for the Lord to displace my own Islamic assumptions and patterns of thought. My father's public confession was as much a beginning as it was a conclusion.

When the freedom of Jesus Christ is proclaimed in a land previously devoted to his enemies, living in that freedom requires the work of reclamation. And a human soul claimed by Christ is a lot like that land. After the celebration ended that evening, I invited my father into a time of repentance — the confession of sin, renunciation of its power, and the embrace of Jesus's rule in every area of former wickedness. Like me, he had to be freed from the chains of false belief, witchcraft, and rebellion. And like me, he had been the cause of great ruin for many others. So as he poured out his confession with tears and brokenness, the joyful freedom of Jesus flooded in. By confessing sin and seeking forgiveness from God and those he had wronged, he became a free man, able to walk in the light. This drive towards the light, towards openness and disclosure before God and his people, is the spirit of the East African Revival.[10] Even more, though, it is the spirit of true Christianity wherever it is found.

---

10. See "'Tukutendereza Yesu' The Balokole Revival in Uganda" by Kevin Ward, in the *Dictionary of African Christian Biography* at www.dacb.org.

EPILOGUE

AS THE SCRIPTURE TEACHES, "If we walk in the light, as he is in the light, we have fellowship with one another, and the blood of Jesus his Son cleanses us from all sin" (1 John 1:7). By coming into the light of Jesus, my father and I were restored to one another in a way that was beyond our imagining when I was child, even when I was the great hope for his future. We have come to something better than a dynasty of sheikhs. Now we have true, everlasting fellowship with one another, cleansed from sin and standing in the glorious goodness of Jesus. It is a relationship, and a path, that he could never have imagined when I was born.

My father was true to his word, and he pursued forgiveness from my mother, and eventually reconciliation: true fellowship in the light. Beyond any hope I had dared hope as a child or even as a grown follower of Jesus, in April of 2016 my father and mother — a former Muslim sheikh and a former priestess of traditional African spirits, a Hutu and a Tutsi — were bound together in Christian marriage at the Anglican Church in Gisenyi. As the Lord said through Joel, "I will restore to you the years that the swarming locust has eaten," so he is now restoring the years consumed by hate, betrayal, bitterness, and malice. He is the redeemer of all things, and he makes all things new.

Along with my younger siblings turn to followings Jesus, my two elder sisters, whom I forced to marry Muslim sheikhs, have also come to know Jesus through difficult circumstances. The eldest sister lives a very hard life, treated like a slave and abused when she shows her faith in Jesus in any outward way. She is not permitted to visit my family or my parents without her husband. The second sister is married to a liberal Muslim who is more interested in keeping up appearances. He does not restrict her movements, but neither does he allow her to join with Christians publicly. Like many Muslims and nominal Christians, keeping the appearance is more import ant than the spiritual reality, and as long as his honor is intact, he cares little for what she believes. The whole family prays for these husbands, and we trust that the Lord in his mercy will work in their hearts as he has worked in ours.

In December of 2015, I was ordained as a deacon in the Anglican Church of Rwanda, and in December of 2016 as a presbyter. Since my conversion, I had never ceased preaching and proclaiming the resurrection power of Jesus Christ, but the Lord had been tempering me, guiding me to a proper place in the ministry of his Church and the advancement of his Kingdom. As a pastor in submission to the Church, I have the strength and support, both relationally and institutionally, of the Fellowship of Confessing Anglicans all over the globe. I have felt and continue to feel the blessing of that unity of mission. I am not just a pastor in Rwanda, but I am a missionary of the global Church wherever I am able to preach.

As a pastor in the Anglican Church of Rwanda, I now lead a congregation in the Kigali Diocese. It is a gracious group of people passionate for the love of Jesus to be made known up and down the hills and valleys of Kanyinya Parish. They are also gracious to be without me on many Sundays throughout the year. I continue to pursue every opportunity for evangelistic preaching outside the parish, at conferences, in prisons, university missions, and open-air events throughout East Africa. Most often, I share parts of the story you have just read, drawing attention to the saving power of Jesus and his willingness to forgive every kind of person and every kind of sin.

My heart and my mission tend to be drawn most powerfully to those caught in the sorts of bondage from which Jesus freed me: Folk Islam and self-destruction through substances. On a recent trip to South Sudan, I was invited by a former classmate from Bishop Barham University to preach the gospel to refugees from Sudan, both Muslims and Christians. The church in South Sudan is growing so rapidly that anyone with a theological education is needed to lead. Even though he's only a young man, my friend has been made a bishop in a remote border region of the country where most of these new Christians have lacked good Bible teaching, so that they continue to be practitioners of traditional African religion. During my visit, we spent time with refuges and with some of the most isolated churches, calling the Christians to walk fully in the light of Jesus and "throw away the foreign gods that are among you and yield your hearts to the Lord" (Joshua 24:23). The work of the Holy Spirit was shown through many people confessing and repenting, publicly burning objects used for practicing witchcraft and engaging spirits.

As Jesus promised, those who hate him also hate those who proclaim him. The principalities and powers of evil respond ferociously when their hold is threatened, especially when they have enjoyed a virtual monopoly on control of a people group. Following several days of ministry, I and my hosts were attacked by a group from one of the rebel factions. They took everything we had and beat us severely. As they were discussing whether to kill us, I was fervently praying the 23rd Psalm, knowing I was again in the valley of the shadow of death. Far away in Rwanda, Dorcus was moved at that moment to pray earnestly for me. But it was not yet time for me to join the Lord. As the rebels decided what to do with us, they concluded it would be dangerous to have the blood of pastors on their hands, so they left us weary and beaten in the wilderness. We struggled and limped eight hours to the nearest settlement. Although we spent several days in the hospital and many days in pain, we truly rejoiced to suffer for the name of Jesus.

Another area of fruitful ministry has been closer to home. In March of 2016, I visited a prison in Kigali at the invitation of the bishop. Through the permission of the government, prisoners are given the opportunity to hear religious messages from specially invited guests, typically messages towards the end of forgiveness and reconciliation. Because I was known for turning from a life of crime, I was given a ready welcome. As I shared my story, I spotted a group of Muslims in the crowd, noticeable by their head caps. There in the group was a young man I had known from the Muslim school in Gisenyi. As I spoke, I prayed inwardly for the Lord to open their hearts to receive the gospel of Jesus. They were all listening with rapt attention as I told of my bondage to sin and drugs, and then my zeal for Islam. When I spoke of my death, the large meeting space was perfectly still. And as I recounted meeting Jesus and returning to my body, eyes were wide and bodies were tense. I shared briefly about the freedom that Jesus brings and the power he gives to overcome sin and bondage to evil. Finally, I concluded by inviting anyone who desired it to receive prayer, confess the rule of Jesus, and ask for his forgiveness.

Among the approximately one hundred men who surrendered to Jesus that day were the five Muslims who constituted the mosque within the prison. Serving as their imam was the man I had known from school. He came rushing up after the message.

"Is it really you? You were my teacher!" Again and again he kept repeating his astonishment, until finally I asked if he also wanted to be free.

At first, his fellow Muslims tried to dissuade him. They reminded him of the cost. "You can't do this," they said. "You can't just turn in an instant."

But the Lord had spoken to his heart, and he had glimpsed life. When he knelt down to proclaim Jesus as Lord, the other four joined him, and together they gave themselves to the King of Kings.

From this initial visit to the prison, Bishop Louis Muvunyi of Kigali has given me many opportunities to return. With the government's consent, he appointed me as chaplain to Kigali's central prison, which now forms a distinct part of my regular ministry. Every time I go, I'm mindful that I could easily have ended my life in such a place.

In addition to speaking the truth of Jesus to nominal Christians and Muslims, I also find myself confronting the more aggressive forces of traditional African religion. In the same month as that first visit to the prison, I was invited to preach for a conference at a rural parish in northern Uganda. It is an area known for the prevalence of African religion. I was warned that a powerful sorcerer who had held sway in the area for many years was planning to come to disrupt the meeting. I made it known that he should come because he will find that Jesus is more powerful than the forces on his side.

When the first meeting began, I saw him arrive at the edge of the crowd wearing an antlered mask, a leopard's skin, and draped with other totems of his magic. As our singing concluded and the time came for me to speak, he began to dance and chant spells. I asked the parish leader to sing another song while I knelt down and prayed. I asked the Lord to move in power, stop this man, and break the power that controlled him. Immediately, he fell down and grew stiff, as if he were dead. I told the brothers to carry him forward and bring him down to the front. While the songs continued, I and other Christians prayed for him and commanded the departure of evil spirits. After some time of battle in this way, the man stood up, confessing that Jesus is truly the Lord of All.

Epilogue

As you can imagine, when the Lord demonstrates his power and might, as well as his mercy — willing to deliver a man who had given himself completely to evil — something profound happens in the spiritual environment. He opens the people to a willingness to receive the gospel in a deeper way. When this sorcerer confessed Jesus as Lord, many people became ready and eager to hear how they could be saved from their own bondage to the darkness. In such a situation, the Lord has already opened the way, and my task is simply to declare his love and willingness to forgive.

On that day, as on other occasions like it, many people responded to the gospel because it was proclaimed with full confidence in the One who opens minds and hearts to receive it. There is no manipulating people into true faith. The Holy Spirit is the one who opens hearts, brings conviction, and sets people free. For us who preach, it is ours simply to state the truth.

Even people who have acknowledged Jesus in some way or have been church attenders, but have held on to various forms of idolatry or paganism, find that with the real Jesus, there can be no "limping between two opinions" (1 Kings 18:21). Like the Israelites on Mt. Carmel when Elijah brought the people to witness a contest with Baal, if the LORD is God, then he must be served. If Jesus is stronger than any other power, and if he is not only strong but also good, there is nothing better than to follow him.

But what I want people to also hear and come to know is that this Jesus, both Lord and Savior, is full of love and kindness. His mercy is new every morning, and if he has saved a man like me who stood against him in every way, he is willing to save anyone who will call on his name. Let the whole earth know it!

GLOSSARY

Akhi: Literally, "my brother." Common way for one Muslim male to refer to another.

Allah: The name for God in Islam.

Al-Lat, Al-Uzza, and Manat: Moon goddesses and the daughters of Allah.

Ba-twa, or Twa: The smallest minority ethnic group in Rwanda, accounting for about 1% of the population. They are a pygmy people who lived traditionally in forest areas as hunter-gatherers. They occupy a socially inferior position in Rwandan society.

Biheko: Traditional East African deity worshipped in parts of Rwanda, Uganda, Burundi, and Congo, and associated especially with fertility.

Dar al-Islam: Literally, "House of Islam." Refers to the parts of the world, including small local communities, living under sharia law. Can also refer simply to the global members of the Islamic faith.

Da'wah: Mission or proselytizing in Islam.

Hadith: Recorded traditions of the prophet Muhammad and his followers, holding the highest authority in Islam after the Qur'an.

Hadj: A pilgrimage to Mecca and one of the Five Pillars of Islam, required of every Muslim once in life.

Hutu: The largest of the three major ethnic groups who settled in Rwanda, comprising just over 80% of the population. Distinct for an agricultural way of life, they were oppressed by the Belgian colonial administration in favor of the Tutsi.

Imam: Spiritual leader and teacher in the local mosque, and leader of the daily prayers.

Injil: The Gospels of the New Testament, as revised in the Qur'an and believed to have been spoken through Jesus.

Interahamwe: Literally, "Those who attack together." Local militias of extremist Hutus organized for the persecution and eventual extermination of the Tutsi minority.

Dying in Islam, Rising in Christ

Islam: "Submission"—the essence of the faith established by Muhammad.

Jamaat: The congregation of a mosque, meaning exclusively the mature males.

Jibril: The archangel Gabriel, said to have delivered some of the Qur'an's revelations to Muhammad.

Jihad: Holy war or struggle, which can be interpreted as physical violence, politics, economics, diplomacy, and/or spiritual struggle.

Jinn: Spirits made by Allah from smokeless fire. They can be either good or evil.

Jumu'ah: Congregational prayer held just after noon on Fridays. Roughly analogous with Christian Sunday morning worship.

Ka'aba: "House of Allah." The ancient black square building in Mecca towards which Muslims turn for prayer. Muslims believe it was built by Abraham and Ishmael. Before consecrated for Allah, it housed the idols of many gods.

Kinyarwanda: The language of Rwandans, including all its ethnic groups.

Kitenge: Long, colorful cloth typically used as a head-wrap by African women.

Kufi: Rounded cap worn by Muslim males.

Kwita Izina: The traditional naming ceremony in Rwandan culture, which includes all the children in a village offering names to the baby's aunts. Occurs about a month after a child's birth.

Manzil: One of the seven equal divisions of the Qur'an.

Mecca: Birthplace of Muhammad in Saudi Arabia. Focal point for the initial conquest of Islam and considered the holiest city in the world.

Mosque: Place of worship for Muslims.

Muezzin: Leader who makes the call to prayer five times each day.

Muhadhara: Organized event for preaching and public debate. The primary method for proselytizing in African Islam.

Muhammad: Fifth century Saudi Arabian who became the founder of Islam, who Muslims believe is the last and greatest prophet.

Muslim: "One who submits to Allah."

Mwami: The title of the King of Rwanda prior to Belgian occupation.

Qur'an : Arabic language collection of Allah's revelations to Muhammad given in several instances over a period of years. The eventual Qur'an was chosen from among many different collections; all others were destroyed. Believed to exactly match a book in Allah's heaven.

Glossary

Ramadan: A month of fasting for Muslims everywhere, observance of which is one of the Five Pillars of Islam. Ninth month in the lunar calendar, the month in which Muhammad's first revelations were given.

Rasta: Short for Rastafarianism, a syncretistic religion developed in the Caribbean that includes elements of Roman Catholicism, African religion, political pan-Africanism, and drug use. Can also refer to the dances that form the major public practice of the religion.

RPF: Rwandan Patriotic Front. A Tutsi army organized within the Ugandan military and led by General Paul Kigame, Rwanda's current President. Its successful invasion in 1994 ended the 100-day genocide of the Tutsis.

Salaat: The five daily prayers or recitations of Islam made towards the Ka'aba, observance of which is one of the Five Pillars of Islam.

Sharia: Islamic law based on the Qur'an and Hadith and necessary for a faithful Muslim to follow.

Shi'ite: Literally, "Followers of Ali." One of the major branches of Islam who believe Muhammad's cousin (and son-in-law) Ali was the true successor to Muhammad.

Sunni: Literally, "People of the Way." One of the major branches of Islam who believe Abu Bakr and Umar were the rightful successors of Muhammad.

Surah: A chapter of the Qur'an.

Thobe: Traditional long, loose robe worn by Muslim males.

Tutsi: One of the two ethnic minorities who settled Rwanda and anciently united the various tribes into a single Rwandan kingdom. Favored by the Belgian colonial administration, they became the object of Hutu animosity after Rwandan Independence in 1962. A genocide of the Tutsi was attempted in 1994, lasting 100 days and resulting in the death of at least 800,000 Tutsis.

☩ GAFCON
GLOBAL ANGLICAN FUTURE CONFERENCE

This book is an indirect result of the Global Anglican Future Conference, which is a movement of renewal within the global Anglican Church of Anglican Christians committed to holding fast to the Bible as the measure of the true Christian faith, and to proclaiming the unchanging, transforming Gospel of Jesus Christ. Responding to a long and steady compromise in morality and doctrine within parts of the Anglican Communion, particularly over issues of biblical authority, over a thousand clergy and lay leaders (representing the majority of the world's Anglicans) gathered in Jerusalem in 2008 and issued the Jerusalem Statement and Declaration, also establishing a permanent leadership council of Archbishops.

Through the GAFCON movement, a united Gospel mission of Anglicans around the world has reaffirmed the received faith of the Church. The powerful witness of Global South churches, often in the face of Islamic terrorism and militant nationalism, has given renewed vigor to Western Anglicans facing more subtle battles with cultural politics and moral decline. Evidence of this influence is apparent in the initial recognition at GAFCON 2008 of the Anglican Church in North America (ACNA) as a member Province of the Anglican Church. Through GAFCON, American Anglicans have direct, intentional relationship with sister churches in the Global South, such as the Anglican Church of Rwanda. The relationship of this book's authors developed through these links between GAFCON churches.

To learn more about GAFCON and the united mission of the Global Anglican Future Conference, go to *www.gafcon.org*. For more information about the mission in America, visit *www.anglicanchurch.net*.

In the precolonial kingdom of Rwanda, the walls of kings' and chiefs' residences were decorated with spiral and geometric designs painted with black, white, and red pigments. Thought to have been invented by Prince Kakira, the son of the king of Gisaka (now known as Kibungo, or the Eastern Province), **imigongo designs** are produced by mixing cow dung with ash, then molding raised geometric patterns that are dried in the sun. Colored paints created by organic material such as plants and clay are then applied to the dry panel. Prior to the 1994 Genocide, the craft was practiced throughout the country, but it was nearly lost due to the conflict. This art was resurrected in 2000 by a local women's cooperative in the village of Nyakarimbi, in the Eastern Province near the border of Tanzania. Named for the art's inventor, the Kakira Imigongo Cooperative now trains a new generation in this traditional art form.

PEMBROKE STREET PRESS

Made in the USA
Lexington, KY
25 September 2018